Mile Post 104 and Beyond

We have walked together in the shadow of the rainbow

ROBERT P. WELLS

Also by Robert P. Wells

Wawahte

Subject: Indian Residential Schools

*The Northern Lights are Spirit Angles
that lift us to our feet when our wings have
trouble remembering how to fly.*

-

As told to Robert P. Wells
By Indian Residential School Survivors

Available now from Trafford Publishing by visiting www.trafford.com
You may order this title at your local bookseller or preferred on-line retailer.
ISBN 978-1-4669-1717-0 (Soft Cover) ISBN 978-1-4669-1719-4 (Hard Cover)
ISBN: 978-1-4669-1718-7(eBook) ISBN: 978-1-4907-0939-0 (Audio Book:

MILE POST 104 AND BEYOND

Life in the Canadian Bush

We Have Walked Together in
the Shadow of the Rainbow

ROBERT P. WELLS

Order this book online at www.trafford.com
or email orders@trafford.com

Most Trafford titles are also available at major online book retailers.

© Copyright 2015 Robert P. Wells.

All rights reserved. No part of this publication may be reproduced, stored in a retrieval system, or transmitted, in any form or by any means, electronic, mechanical, photocopying, recording, or otherwise, without the written prior permission of the author.

Print information available on the last page.

ISBN: 978-1-4907-5538-0 (sc)
ISBN: 978-1-4907-5537-3 (e)

Because of the dynamic nature of the Internet, any web addresses or links contained in this book may have changed since publication and may no longer be valid. The views expressed in this work are solely those of the author and do not necessarily reflect the views of the publisher, and the publisher hereby disclaims any responsibility for them.

Any people depicted in stock imagery provided by Thinkstock are models, and such images are being used for illustrative purposes only.
Certain stock imagery © Thinkstock.

Trafford rev. 06/10/2015

Trafford PUBLISHING   www.trafford.com
North America & international
toll-free: 1 888 232 4444 (USA & Canada)
fax: 812 355 4082

CONTENTS

Dedication vii
Epigraph ix
Introduction to the Beyond xiii

The Day Jacky Got Born 1
104 Miles to Mid-Century 3
Life Along the Railway 7
Windigoostigwan Time & The Black Hornets 11
- Learning – Jimmy Clock Time 11
- Time Management Issues 13
- The Black Hornets 15

A Boy Becomes a Hunter 17
The Fourth Penny 23
Friendship Has No Boundaries 25
Phillip Sawdo Cries 34
Trapper, Bob Sawdo 38
Lilly's Plane Crash 41
Living the Bush Life 44
Our Wedding Day 48
Home and Family 50
Our First Snowmobile.. 52
Do you have running water in the winter?................. 54
Putting some Balance in our Lives............................... 56
Friends & Neighbours.. 58
- The Chicago Family... 59
- The Peters Family 61

Jack's Secrets and Dreams 62
Thrown to the Bear 68
Time to Move On 71
"Tower Man" – Inge Wells 72
A Conservation Officer Looks Back 75
Why Did the Coyotes Move to Town? 78
Natural Resources - Beyond Biological Management 82
Russia – 1993 86
My Greatest Teachers 92
The Last Period 96

Acknowledgements 99

DEDICATION

Bob and Kay

Bobby – Jimmy – Jacky – George

Windy –> A World . . .

⬇

You Matter. You Are Important. You Belong.

EPIGRAPH

We have walked together in the shadow of the rainbow

One summer's afternoon we gathered on our sand beach to greet Mrs. Sawdo and to admire her newly-crafted birch-bark canoe. This Ojibwa lady looked in astonished awe on seeing a baby porcupine nestled against my neck and said,

"Bobby-boy, you and your porcupine friend walk together in the shadow of a rainbow[1]."

---

[1] This Native American saying depicts surreal happenings between wild animals and people.

Gerard Wyatt, Professor Emeritus, Queen's University at Kingston

In this collection of stories, Bob Wells brings us some glimpses, both insightful and entertaining, of a Canada that was. He grew up at his parents' fishing lodge near Quetico, in North-Western Ontario, accessible at that time only by rail. His familiar surroundings were the lakes and the forests, and his childhood companions were his three younger brothers and the few people living in the area, chiefly of Aboriginal or recent immigrant stock. His early formal schooling was somewhat intermittent, but by the age of 11, his hunting was providing meat for his family. He was invited by a Doctor and his wife to join their home in Milwaukee, where he attended school. For five years, Bob spent winters with them, returning to the lake for summers, to guide tourists who came to fish. He married Inge, recently from Germany; they spent seven winters, running a Trapline, raised a son, and remain companions to the present time. After obtaining the necessary formal qualification, Bob served as an Ontario Conservation Officer and enjoyed a career being paid for doing what he liked to do. Taking an early retirement, Bob and Inge settled in Kingston, after living in Georgia for five years. He participates in many community activities and escapes to the nearby lakes and woods to refresh his contact with nature and stock their larder with fish and venison. Bob is distinguished by his intimate knowledge of, and respect for, Aboriginal Peoples, the natural environment, along with his warm personality and ability to make and keep friends. Already in boyhood, he was clearly a curious listener that encouraged others to share their personal stories.

INTRODUCTION TO THE BEYOND

The Author
Robert P. Wells

My father, Robert (Bob) Vincent Wells (Dupuis), originally from New Brunswick, was a Quetico Provincial Park Ranger from 1927 to 1941. He met my mother Katherine (Kay) Carol, a Registered Nurse, while in a hospital in Two Harbours, Minnesota. They married in 1934 and I arrived two years later.

In 1938, my parents purchased property on Windigoostigwan (Windy) Lake in North-Western Ontario from Professor Frank

Buck, an uncle to author Pearl S. Buck. Here they went on to build Wells' Fishing Lodge, a remote mid-twentieth-century fishing tourist lodge, guest cabins and service buildings. In time, American doctors, automotive executives and businessmen were arriving and leaving weekly by train. Exceptionally good fishing, home cooked meals, kerosene lamps, outhouses and good service brought "tourists" back year after year to fish and or hunt.

Wells' Fishing Lodge, Quetico, at Mile Post 104 was my boyhood home. Mile Post 104 denoted the miles of Canadian National Railroad track between Thunder Bay and home.

Our family consisted of my mom and dad, three younger brothers, myself, and sometimes an uncle. In winter, we might have an occasional visitor, but that was rare. Each time someone visited it was an event appreciated as the rarity that it was. We lived in relative solitude close to nature; we heard the smallest of noises and very little went unnoticed. To see people, whom we had not seen before, was to watch the CNR passenger train pass. Some of the people would wave back. The train did not stop unless my dad had a reason for it to do so. There were no roads or automobiles. I never met children who lived less than twenty miles away.

When I went out of doors, my catechism lessons remained at home with my morally religious mom. My spirit was seized by the wonders of nature, my Aboriginal friends' cultural concept of life, and interconnections with the natural world.

I learned that there were times when what you are thinking is better left unsaid. For example: when you are eight years of age, with your mother and grandmother present, never-ever debate with the twice-yearly visiting Jesuit priest "that animals are kindred beings with spirits and are to be respected – people are not the boss". That is, unless you want to hear *"Bobby, you made your grandmother and me so embarrassed."* Ouch! Dad came to my emotional rescue, when outside he gave me a love-tap (knock-on-the-head) saying; "That was so funny - ha, ha, ha – you had them sputtering in there. Be-jesses-boy you stood your ground".

My parents permitted me the independence to wander, free from fear, and oblivious of racial, religious and ethnic prejudices so prevalent in the day. Becoming everyone's regular drop-in-visitor, my dog Bernie at my side and .22-calibre rifle in hand, I roamed wherever my legs would take me.

My dad encouraged me to tell him whom I visited and what I had seen in my travels. He particularly liked me telling him funny things that people said or did. Such fun! He'd often say, "Bobby, don't give everything you shoot away unless you think folks have no meat in their house to eat. Our family dinner table depends on you."

Debatably, me going to school one week out of five on the School Car was a waste of time. My brother, John, who had not yet begun school, mostly solved my homework problem. He did most of my home studies well enough to get me passing grades. My hunting prowess put 85% of the meat on the family dinner table.

If it were not for receiving magazines I would have grown up believing the world flat, and, if I wandered too far that I would fall over the edge and become lost forever.

Summer tourist season responsibilities slowed my wanderings. With parental permission, I could take tourists fishing. As long as it did not appear that I was acting as a guide. Such was the case when I 'went-fishing' with Chicago Rabbi Sam and his grandson Isaac. Isaac, my age, liked to operate the outboard motor and to help me prepare our shore-lunch of fried fish. To qualify for a $2.00 Ontario Guides Licence, you had to be sixteen years of age.

My mother took great pride having the Governor of her home state, Minnesota, the "Land of 10,000 Lakes", come to our fishing lodge. He was not a return client because of political condemnation for leaving his state to fish. Then there was Mr. Clark Gable, the star of the movie Gone With The Wind. His last minute cancellation put all fourteen of the community into a state of downheartedness. Not having ever seen a movie, I was somewhat mystified by all the fuss. Neighbours planned to greet Mr. Gable as he stepped off the train. My mother kept this missed event alive for years. When worried about a lull in the business she would say, "This would not be happening had Clark Gable come. He would have made our lodge famous, and we would be full at all times." Who knows, she may have been right!

When I was 15 years of age, Dr. John Dale and Jean Owen invited me to come live with them in Milwaukee, Wisconsin. On the seven hundred mile drive to what became my winter home for five years, I saw the world not to be flat, and, in a store window, saw television for the first time. Wow!

Reflecting back, I never sensed that people here were attempting to change me... Save me, yes! I did receive academic skills and the confidence to dream (think) the attainable. My dreams and ambitions differed from most of my classmates at Shorewood High School, Milwaukee, Wisconsin. Football, achieving excellent grades, parties, and going off to Yale or Harvard to become doctors or lawyers, were not my dream. The Owens, their friends, and my teachers at Shorewood High School went the 'extra-mile' to help me assimilate and feel welcomed into a culture much different from my life in the Canadian bush. I graduated high school in 1956. I was one of the first in my father's ancestral branch of our four-hundred-year Acadian history to do so.

My brother Jim joined me my second year and became a member of the Owen family for ten years. He graduated from the

University of Wisconsin and served in the U.S. Army for 25 years. He retired in 1988 at the rank of Colonel. Jim died in 2012.

Waiting for the Train
Jim (age 12), Dr. John Dale and Jean Owen and me (age 16)

Our family tourist lodge lost business after the construction of the highway from Thunder Bay to Atikokan. Once people could drive to the lake, we no longer maintained our attraction as a wilderness experience destination

Selling the lodge, I moved on: guided fishers and moose hunters, trapped fur, fought forest fires, and served a twenty-eight and a half year career as an Ontario Conservation Officer. At the time of this writing, I have been retired for twenty-two years.

THE DAY JACKY GOT BORN . . .

I was four and a half years old the day Jacky got born. I don't remember much of anything else that happened to me that year, except the day Jacky got born. I have no recollection of knowing that such an event was about to take place until early one January morning in 1941. My Aunt Julia had spent the night at our house and Mrs. Tenniscoe and Russell came when it was still dark.

Mommy told me that today she had to be in bed. She was waiting there for the stork to bring me a baby brother or sister and for me to stay with Russell and watch for the stork.

Why? I already had a brother Jimmy, who was three days less than one year old, and I did not want a baby sister. What I wanted was a real gun, a puppy, and my kitty, Boots, to come home. [Years later I learned why Boots had "run-away" – Caught in a bear-trap.] We are getting a new baby because God wants our family to have one. Why didn't God ask me? We don't need another stupid baby; we already have Jimmy.

Daddy knew this was going to happen and that is why he left a week ago to go someplace far away. I should have gone with him. Jimmy was crying and he didn't even know why. Russell put a chair on the kitchen table so I could see out the window and watch for the stork. Russell and Aunt Julia agreed that it would be all right for me to shoot the stork with my slingshot. Maybe I can put a stop to all this. Russell even gave me two of his prettiest marbles for my slingshot as there was snow on the ground and I had shot away all the rocks I had collected before winter came.

I heard my Mommy cry out and then a baby cry. I said a bad word that I had heard my Daddy say. How could that x*@X stork bring a baby to our house and me not see him? Finally, I was making such a fuss that I was allowed in to see Mommy and my new baby brother. Mommy looked kind of funny and my newborn brother looked all red and wrinkly. The stork had hurt my Mommy when he dropped him on her tummy. I don't think that I am going to like my new baby brother. I want a real gun, a puppy and Boots to come home. I am glad I did not get a baby sister. Well, if God wanted our family to have a new baby, I guess it is OK, but I want to be the first to tell Daddy when he comes home. Boy, is he going to be surprised. I think that this was my first *"worst day of my life."*

I am now happy that I didn't shoot the stork the day Jacky got born. Thank you, Stork, for you brought me a great, intelligent, unique, original thinker of a brother. The world would have been less without him. Jimmy grew up to be, Jim, who was not stupid, and Jacky became, John.

A few years later, God sent us George. This time Mom went to the hospital to pick him up. It had been more fun doing it the other way. Oh, really!

104 MILES TO MID-CENTURY

Windigoostigwan Lake view of Wells' Fishing Lodge

The Wells' family life in the 1940s was typical of isolated country living. Granted, we had radio, which worked when we could afford a battery, steam locomotives to draw trains, and gasoline-powered outboard motors. Water, we carried in a pail from the lake, cut and burned firewood for cooking and warmth, took out the ashes, and threw our garbage in a garbage hole . . . Mom washed our clothes on a scrub board and hung the wash on outdoor clothes lines. In winter, she would wear snowshoes to hang the wash for it to frost-dry. It took two days to frost-dry at -10º F. and longer at warmer temperatures. We took Saturday night baths in laundry tubs, relieved ourselves in chamber pots or outhouses — not a place to sit and ponder in the winter.

With the exception of food staples such as, tea, coffee, milk, flour, bacon, sugar, and oranges[2], we provided for ourselves. We kept chickens, raised pigs, grew vegetables, gathered, fished, and hunted. I have no memory of ever going hungry. Almost everyone smoked. Father once walked twenty miles across a lake on the glare ice wearing boot cleats to get cigarettes.

When sick or injured we were better off than most since mother was a registered nurse. She and her medicine bag were often called out to attend to the sick and injured neighbours. She performed medical procedures reserved to that of licensed physicians. *"I'll do what I must to save a person's life . . . and I did".*

Tracks in the snow told the story of wildlife and the comings and goings of our neighbours. We knew everyone and their personal business thanks, in part, to our party line telephone. Except for seeing people we did not know, who were riding the passenger train, it was not unusual for a winter to pass without seeing a single stranger. We talked with, and about, our neighbours. Mostly the talk was about wildlife activities and what it might be like to live in places shown in magazine pictures.

At about age eleven, I became interested in Africa, which came to an abrupt end when Mom burnt *my special interest*, ladies-without-shirts, National Geographic Magazines. Would I ever learn? I only asked her — why were black ladies shown in books without shirts and white ladies not? My dad said, "It was just plain stupid to ask your mother something like that".

The Sears and Eaton catalogue toy section pages would be worn thin long before Christmas. No wonder Santa Claus only brought a couple of the things my brothers and I wanted; he could not see the pages of our Christmas wish books for all the request

---

[2] Dad said, "We must eat oranges to prevent "the scurv" scurvy, the curse of winter".

pencil check marks. At least, my brothers did not blame me for Santa shorting them on Christmas gifts. I did get blamed for snaring and shooting "Easter Bunny Helpers," and for them not getting all the candy in the world.

Once each winter mother and kids traveled the one hundred and four miles by train to Port Arthur – (Thunder Bay) – awesome experiences. My brothers' faces were pressed against the train windows each time that there was something to see other than trees and lakes. After one such excursion, my brothers Jim and John argued for days about what colour car could go the fastest.

Dad's patience was stretched to the limit by hearing . . . "I saw a green car going faster than a black car". He hollered out, in lumberjack talk, "Jumping-Jesus-Christ, you stupid little bastards, it's just the colour of the paint, which has nothing to do with how fast a car can go". It got real quiet, except for Mother, saying words that had nothing to do with which colour car is the fastest. An educational moment! I learned that we were not bastards as Dad so often said we were – Mother, angrily reminded him that her children had married parents . . . Yikes!

When we stayed in town we must have driven our town friends nearly out of their minds; examining the magic of light switches and trying to make the whirlpool in the toilet twist the other way. Their houses had no wood box, yet the house was made warm by a big stove in the basement that burned black lumps of coal. Needing a drink, which we always did, all you had to do was turn a tap — careful, not too fast —"How many times do we have to tell you kids that?" The bathtub was big enough for two or three of us to fit in all at once. Going to the store every day was also a new and wonderful experience. At the lodge our groceries arrived once a month by train.

So many people that seemed to be going nowhere in a hurry. Most passed each other on the sidewalk without nodding or saying hello . . . Why? Some of the sights were just like the pictures in the magazine. Many great topics for another round of endless arguing! The promise of going to the store for ice cream or being threatened with being sent to bed provided the adults with moments of near quiet.

As much as we enjoyed "going to town", coming home was also wonderful even though we usually ended up having colds, the mumps, chicken pox, measles or some other nasty childhood illness.

LIFE ALONG THE RAILWAY

'The Quetico Section Men'

The romantic days of railroading have become 'steam-locomotives' parked in city squares and the 'heroes' of a nostalgic song. I write this in special tribute to the women I knew... The wives of the Section Men that worked on the railroad and the women who pioneered Canada, and elsewhere, in isolation... Unsung heroes of times past?

Wasalena Kopechanski – Nellie Penko – Miranda Wladichuk

The inaccessible remoteness of their homes and the long winters gave cause for these women to endure great loneliness. For the most part, they were imprisoned in their homes, remote from other women, while their men worked alongside other men out-of-doors.

In the 1940s, Quetico was one of many isolated railroad communities that dotted the map at twelve-mile intervals across Canada. Quetico, like many such places, was not accessible by road. These hamlets, known as Section Points, were usually home to two or three families, in our area they were mostly first-generation Ukrainian immigrants responsible for railway maintenance and service.

I write about these women in tribute to my mother and to my adventurous wife, Inge, who spent seven winters with me on the Trapline. Unlike the Ukrainian ladies, my mother and Inge were able to understand and enjoy radio and occasional visits from the native community. In the summer months, we hosted many people (tourists) who came, mostly from the United States, to fish in Canada.

As a boy riding the night passenger train, I would see faces pressed against windows of the houses we passed, and hands waving to the people on the train. I remember how excited my middle-aged Ukrainian lady friends were when, as a kid; I knocked on their doors; and, their *kindness*. Immediately they would set a table with delicious food not seen in my home, and then tearfully show me tattered letters and pictures of their families back in the 'old country'. Communication was sometimes difficult, but I always departed feeling good about these visits, and, their parting words, "You come back soon – Bobby – bring your little dog Bernie". Mrs. Kopechanski would learn one or two words of English, and me, one or two words of the Ukrainian language. We were *friends*!

We can only guess of the loneliness and despair of these people. They had packed up a few cherished possessions, leaving behind family and friends forever, to sail across the ocean in search of a better life in Canada. During the World War II years, people rarely received letters from their "old country". When, in some miraculous way, a letter did get through, it would be passed from family to family and talked about for months.

The winters were long, cold, and lonely; however, these women maintained dignity and stoic pride in who they were and from where they had come. I truly believe these people were unsung heroes of their time and now. They unselfishly gave so much of themselves for the future of their children.

I am forever grateful to my parents for letting me roam and to be free to associate with people different from us. The descendants of my long-ago friends and others like them, who sacrificed in many ways, have much to be proud of. Names like Penko, Kopechanski, Pecaranuk and Antoniuk were important to my boyhood and are well remembered.

ROBERT P. WELLS

Quetico Station Section Forman Mike Penko – Family and Friends Celebrated the 1st July with a ride on a Handcar.

– 1946 –

WINDIGOOSTIGWAN TIME & THE BLACK HORNETS

Jacky, Bobby & Jimmy Wells
Mother's Angels – Dad's "You Little Bastards"

Learning – Jimmy Clock Time . . .

Teaching five-year-old Jimmy how to read a clock was an opportunity to have some 'devilish' fun with our parents. Several times a week I would get it started by purposely explaining to Jimmy the incorrect meaning of the big hand, the little hand, and the numbers on the clock. Without fail, Mom, and then Dad, would step in and take over the lesson, giving up an hour or so later, completely frustrated because *Jimmy* could never quite grasp the concept. We kept this charade going for what seemed to be weeks. Our scam met with an abrupt end one morning when Mom overheard the two of us plotting out the day's strategy.

Our life went from giggles to bad real fast. Mom came out from a secret meeting with Dad, and began packing us each a suitcase. Dad again, declared us to be "Little Bastards" that got him in trouble with Mom – *"How many times must I tell you that our children parents are married"*. That aside, we were told that they had had enough of the two of us and that we would be leaving on tomorrow morning's train. I would be going to a reform school, or an Indian residential school, seen to be about the same as a reform school, and Jimmy would be going off to somewhere far away to receive electric shocks to his brain and to get a frontal lobotomy. Even though we didn't know the meaning of these big words, including the word electric, it all sounded like trouble. Mom wrote two letters saying what was to be done to the two of us.

The revelation that Jimmy, from the get-go, could tell time as well as any trainmen did not help. Jimmy being able to tell, or not, tell time was no longer an issue. The decision was final; we were going. We spent a sleepless night sobbing and praying that God would come to our rescue by wrecking the train. We were so desperate that we even called upon the Aboriginal Windigo Devil Spirit to save us. No one was listening – including our parents.

The long night passed and that dreadful morning came. Mom prepared us a farewell breakfast that we ate, not because we were hungry, but to show how good we had become. Our pleading even went so far as to be **nice to our little brothers**. Our tearful pleadings included telling them how much **they were going to miss us**. Nothing worked. All too soon, two tender-aged *"Little Bastards"*, with suitcases in hand, were walking up the trail to board the train to 'horrible'. As we heard the train approaching, I detected a glimmer of hope in Jimmy's face and tearful eyes. Our father; who art in heaven I hope, failed to light the green and white lanterns to signal the train to stop – we got a last minute **conditional**

reprieve. Dad made us promise that we would never, ever, again make fun of him by our foolish pretending. "I am not so *goddamn* stupid not to be able to teach someone how to tell time – you Little Bastards". Bless Dad for his lumberjack talk, as it once again, shifted Mom's attention from us to him – *"Thou shall not take the name of the Lord in vain".*

What our parents did not truly appreciate, was that four-year-old Jacky learned to tell time in the process. I am quite sure, that six-month-old George could tell time if only he could talk.

Dad never quite forgave Jim for his toying mind-games, which made him feel like a fool – "All I was trying to do was to teach 'the Little Bastard' how to tell time which he already knew how to do." The other sensitive topic was our "Black Hornet" incident – *but later!*

Time Management Issues

Train Time was not arbitrary. Dad wanted people to consider his time needs as if it were Train Time. However, his time schedule often came in conflict with what we came to call "Indian-Time" or "Why-Now-Time?"

Dad's terms of employment for fishing guides were that they were to wash and ready the boats Saturday mornings in preparation for our incoming Sunday evening guests; very seldom would this happen.

The guides typically came Saturday mornings to bid departing guests farewell but would go nowhere near the boats to wash them. They concluded nobody needed the boats until

Monday, so why not wash and ready them later in the day or maybe on Sunday.

Dad came up with a devious plan to deal with "Indian-Time" boat cleaning. His plan was for me to remain in camp. When I heard the train coming and there was no chance of the departing guests returning to their cabins, I was to run through their cabins and pick up the part bottles of whiskey and wine and hide them in the warehouse. I'd then run up to our train station and quietly tell him how much I had found.

After the train had departed, Dad would say that the tourists had left some liquid-thank-you. And, as he did not drink, he would give it to the guides after the boats were cleaned. It worked every time — the boats were clean and ready to go before noon.

Some of the cocktails Dad prepared and gave those guys must have been nothing less than terrible – but **good**. He would pour whatever I recovered into one or two bottles, e.g., wine, scotch, vermouth, whiskey . . . Dad's boats got cleaned according to Bob's time!

"Indian-Time" makes sense. For example, we rang a dinner bell to announce mealtimes. My friends would joke, "There goes the bell, telling me that I am hungry, and I must eat." Simply put; why not eat when you are hungry and not at Clock-Time? Or, why paddle across the lake into a strong head wind at three o'clock in the afternoon, when the lake is calm in the evening?

The legendary Windigo Devil Spirit may have influenced our behaviour. Lake Windigoostigwan was our life-support as it was from here that we carried our water, fished, swam and traveled upon.

Windigoostigwan Lake is part of an ancient water travel route. One that Canada's First Peoples used long before European explorers, settlers, and the military came on the scene. Native Elders' oral histories told me that ancestors traveled these waters, but would never live or camp on the lakeshore because of legendary accounts of Windigo Devil beings and evil happenings. As proof, we never found pottery shards or arrowheads, as we often did on other lakes, along the water-travel-route.

You, well-meaning child psychologists, may conclude that we were being subjected to harsh disciplines. Please put your mind at ease, it was just the opposite. It was always about (turnabout) mind games. We were resilient and it wasn't long before we again created opportunities to mess with our parents, each other, or unsuspecting visitors. It helped make the long winter pass quickly. Just maybe, the Windigo did possess the spirit of Windigoostigwan (*Windy*) Lake and toyed with the children who drank its water.

The Black Hornets

It all began early one June when some black hornets selected a low hanging branch of a tree along the trail to the Wells' Fishing Lodge railroad station platform to build their nest. Summer progressed and the hornets' numbers increased and their nest became bigger and bigger. We, in turn, gave it a wider and wider berth going to and from the station. By September, the nest was about the size of a chamber pot. It was then that we took it upon ourselves to destroy it.

Jimmy, the self-appointed expedition leader at age five and a half, Jackie, a year younger and me, age eight, set off up the trail late one afternoon. We tried to destroy the nest by throwing rocks. Our aim was poor and we could not hit the nest. Never to be deterred, our leader Jimmy, stick in hand and against my advice, knocked the nest to the ground with a single swat. What ensued was an instant swarm of very mad stinging hornets.

This, by chance, occurred as Dad came walking down the pathway carrying a metal lunch box, the kind that workmen once used. Hearing screams and him thinking that a bear was attacking his three "Little Bastards", he ran to the rescue. True to Dad's ways, he later said, "As soon as I stumbled over the nest I grabbed screaming Jimmy off the ground as he was being swarmed by hornets. All the while I was **swatting the stinging black bastards on my head with my goddamn lunch pail.** I ran us into the lake where we both nearly drowned – *Jumping-Jesus-Christ!*"

While this was happening I grabbed little Jackie as we were also being stung and took off running. Mom said that she could not believe her eyes when the four of us appeared. She said, "It was just *awful* to see my three kids, each with multiple hornet stings, and Bob who looked as if he had been struck by a train and thrown into the lake".

Swatting black hornets with his lunch pail had cut Dad up so badly that Mom had to stitch his wounds. Having our own first aid issues we quickly decided it best not to hang around and watch. Dad was angry enough that he wanted to kill Jimmy and me – but mostly Jimmy! Fortunately, he had to stay in bed for three days to recuperate from his self-inflected injuries and the wasp stings – this helped to reduce his anger. Joking aside, Mom hid Jimmy for several days, as Dad was prone to having anger flare-ups, which he did without warning! He stayed mad for easily a month, and it took years before he could find it in himself to laugh, *just a little bit*, about our *"black hornet incident"*.

A BOY BECOMES A HUNTER

Once upon a time in the 1940s, a little boy, obsessed with becoming a hunter, was given his very own .22 calibre single-shot Remington rifle. Wow! But not before age ten was he allowed to go hunting alone. I was that little boy. That was the year that I learned more about the skills of deer hunting than since.

My father was one of my greatest teachers. I learned a great deal from him; but he was not my only teacher. With my home-schooled assignments completed I was free to roam the woods and to visit my friend Moochum Joe. ["Moochum" is Grandfather in the Cree language.] Though professing to hate white men, Moochum spent countless afternoons in conversation with me. He taught me, a blond-haired and blue-eyed white kid, the ways of the forest spirits, honour and respect, and the skills of the "great" subsistence hunter.

Showing Moochum Joe my collection of Beaver Magazine clippings about "Indians," he said, "Nabis (boy), your spirit is different from the other white kids I know. You have been given the spirit to one day *draw words on paper* to tell your kind how badly Indian people are being treated. They take our kids away. They do not allow us to live as the people we are. They treat us as children, telling us what and when to do things. They even sell me a child's ticket to ride the train – I am not a child – I am an old man that resents being treated as a child. You should not think of such things now because your journey is still young. When you become older you will know the words. *Draw them true."* [3]

I was a kid with a storybook life. Home-schooled assignments completed; I was free to roam the woods and visit my friend Moochum Joe. Moochum lived alone in a small, dilapidated log cabin on the shore of a small lake next to the railway tracks. He spent countless afternoons teaching this blond-haired blue-eyed kid the secrets of legendary subsistence hunters, and so much more. Each visit began as the last. As Moochum was then very old and unable to venture more than a short distance from his cabin, I would fill his wood box and carry water from the nearby lake. Then we would have tea and he would smoke a cigarette that I had pinched from my parents. His counsel was about how one must respect oneself, ancestors, nature, the spirits, the animals you hunt, and the importance of sharing your successes with a friend.

Moochum would often say, "Me learn boy hunter our old ways. You have a good little gun. Big guns and trains make too much noise, make Windigo mad". Windigos are highly respected, feared, native devil-beings. I soon learned that my 'one-God-one-Devil' parents did not want to learn about the forest spirits or native spirituality. To their great credit, my parents, never in any way tried to stop to me in this pursuit; that was as long as I could *recite* my catechism lessons.

My mentoring in hunter stealth and concealment was in the form of 'songs' – stories that strongly emphasized consequences. Never was hunting talked about as sport but as something we do to live and to be proud – *a way of life*. Moochum's teachings have taken me a lifetime to comprehend.

---

[3] Sixty-five years later we published the book "Wawahte" (Audio Book and Educational Documentary) the subject of Canadian Indian Residential Schools – from the perspective of three survivors.

MILE POST 104 AND BEYOND

Hunting has always been important to me. Here are some of the main points that I have learned:

- Smell – Hunters get off to a bad start by disregarding wind direction when entering the woods. Remember how the whole neighbourhood could smell the skunk that got run over even after it was picked up? Scent pockets linger for a long time.

- Noise – Make yourself sound as natural as your immediate surroundings. Animals hear extremely well, so if you do make noise, then remain very quiet until they are no longer on alert.

- Movement – Trust your original decision and stay put. Move only when you can't see the animal's eyes. If you must move to raise your weapon then do so when an animal is moving or when there is a screen of grass or brush between you. Always be aware that another deer may catch your movement and sound the alarm.

- Shine – In the woods, a shaven white face shines like the rising of a full moon. We must try to manage the possible reflection of eyeglasses and other things that we bring to the field.

- Shape – I'm convinced that some wildlife recognizes the human shape.

- Silhouette – Your best camouflage gear will do little to conceal if you project above the horizon or make a sharp contrast with your background.

- Colour – Dark coloured clothing is not easily seen. There is wonderful gear on the market. If you can't afford a suit for every situation then choose a hiding place in the woods that has similar colour and texture to your clothing.

Hunting large animals with a .22 calibre firearm is illegal in most jurisdictions. A .22 calibre bullet entering a deer's body cavity will leave little or no blood trail, which will make tracking extremely difficult. Moochum's counsel was to "Hide, wait and make a perfect shot".

Over sixty years of hunting has left me with many good memories but none more memorable than when I shot the "biggest deer in the world", or so I thought when I was eleven years old. After one year's experience of hunting alone and shooting two small deer, finding a large rub and scrape put all of Moochum's teaching to the test. I waited in ambush, with my little dog Bernie, only on the days when upwind access to our moss and twig covered rock crevice was possible. Amazingly, after several days, Bernie, lying by my side, quietly alerted me to a cautiously approaching eleven-point buck. I can still feel Bernie's quiet but quivering excitement and hear my heart pounding as I aimed my rifle at a spot just below the deer's ear.

In a solemn moment of respect, I offered the Spirits the little bag of tobacco that Moochum gave me for this momentous occasion. I reverently thanked the deer for giving his life to feed my family and friends. Bernie was turning cartwheels, anxious to run home and tell of our deed. Dad brought the horse to drag the biggest deer he had ever seen home. From this time on, "his boy became a man".

I gave Moochum a share of the meat, which according to my parents, was much too large. I told him every detail of the before, during and just after. He, in turn, ceremonially presented me with a badge of accomplishment, his much *cherished* big black feather.

Regrettably, that feather, Moochum, my dog Bernie, and the others are long gone. However, their friendship, love, counsel and teachings remain strong in the heart of the little boy hunter who now has grown old.

After a recent hunting excursion my friend Greg said, "Every day we hunt we learn or relearn something and all too often hunters miss what it was, or do not heed the lesson". My old friend had said, "Good hunter use sneaky skills not luck". However, it has taken me a lifetime to come to understand the most valued lessons of Moochum's counsel:

- "Hunting is not an intellectual or ethical exercise, but a way of life."

- I listened to Moochum Joe relate integrated cultural history in the context of hunting stories, my only real interest at the time. I have now come to understand that there were philosophical perspectives behind the value-laden journeys travelled, which used hunting as the hook to hold my attention.

I now know that my Elder 'teachings' were indigenous cultural values, as well as specific practical knowledge quite different from that of our western cultures. Aboriginal cultures evolved over thousands of years. Many of these people view plants, animals, and nonliving entities such as the moon, sun, wind, water, hills, marsh, and rocks as kindred beings. Kindred beings with human-like traits, often viewed as having special relative status. Shown proper respect, they will give of themselves so that we humans may live.

'Hunting is not an intellectual or ethical exercise but a way of life'

THE FOURTH PENNY

One day, before Canadian pennies were taken out of circulation, I watched teenage boys throwing them about on a shopping mall floor. This seemingly nonsensical act brought back memories of my family's desperate search for 'one' penny.

We awoke to the eerie silence that often follows a violent winter storm. Having been confined inside for three days, my three younger brothers and I looked forward to getting out-of-doors. However, this was not to be. Mom had spent the previous kid-quiet night writing a letter to her mother who lived in Minnesota, only to find that she was short one cent for the four-cent postage stamp required to mail her letter.

Well, before breakfast, we all found ourselves caught up in a frenzied search for just one penny. It was not until late in the morning before Mom called an end to the search. She put my brothers to work shovelling the path to the outhouse, which was now obliterated by snow. I was sent off to borrow a penny from Mr. Penko, the local Post Master and Railroad Section Foreman. Although my little dog was not by my side because of the deep snow, off I went on the one-mile, snowshoe hike through the woods and down the railroad track to Quetico. Mr. and Mrs. Penko and Mr. and Mrs. Kopochonski were the only Quetico residents although other people did live scattered throughout the bush. We measured the distance to neighbouring homes or places, in miles and/or time. The miles or time that it took to walk or paddle a canoe to our destination.

It was my mother's pride that made me having to borrow a penny from Mr. Penko difficult for her. In the early years, most of our money came from operating a small fishing lodge in the summer. To fill in the gap, Father worked away from home most winters. We always had plenty to eat; however, most money went into building the business and paying bills. My hunting provided meat for our table. Neighbours too were happy to see me, and my little dog Bernie, walking up their paths with a snowshoe hare or grouse in hand. No one had much, but what we had, we shared.

Mr. Penko was happy for two of the four grouse I'd shot on my walk from home. He asked me to shoot 'Gaud-damn-weasel' that killed his chicken that was now in the soup pot. Arriving at the barn, with strict instructions from Mrs. Penko, *"You no shoot cow"*, I saw the weasel's head sticking out of the snow. Often told that I was a 'very good shot', I surprised myself when my bullet just nicked the end of the weasel's nose causing no damage to its pelt. Mr. Penko, in heavenly Ukrainian accented English, *"Gaud-damn you shoot good – more good than man solder"*. As usual, I returned home well fed, treats for my little brothers, and a weasel with a pelt worth four dollars.

Two weeks later, when my Father came home, I returned to Mr. Penko the borrowed penny and one dollar from the sale of the weasel pelt. He promised me four free haircuts. Such was life, as I once knew it to be. A chocolate bar then cost five cents.

FRIENDSHIP HAS NO BOUNDARIES

'Friend,' Oxford Dictionary defined: "mutual affection, regard, ally, sympathizer, patron; a romantic or sexual partner; an acquaintance, to be on good terms with." This general definition says very little about the human need for friendship. I cannot imagine life without friends.

The people I write about are my friends. Grandson Jordan, at the time age nine years, and I was fishing one August afternoon when we came upon a raft of eight loons. I told Jordan that when I see or hear loons it makes me think of my Dad. Jordan asked, "Do you miss your Dad?" "Yes, but not in a sad way if this is what you ask. What I miss is his company. He was very comical, and I continue to chuckle at his antics." A few moments of silence had passed before Jordan asked, "Grandpa, what do you think happens to us when we die?" I thought it best to ask Jordan, who attended a parochial school, what he thought. After a long ~~~~ pause

"Grandpa, I believe that when you die that you are dead and that you live on in the hearts of the people who love you."

Consider Jordan's words as you may — this was the first time in my life that I began to understand my feelings about my departed family and friends. They live on in my heart. It is for that reason that I mostly write about people in our time together.

Besides my birth, my mother gave me the greatest gift of all, my childhood freedom to associate with people of my choosing. Not the rule for parents at the time. People tended to keep to their kind and shielded their children from people seen to be different; in particular, if they were of a different religious, ethnic, or cultural background than their own. I remain forever grateful.

My unconstrained childhood made it possible for me to cultivate relationships that most people never experience. I am not sure if all or any of this fits your definition of a friend; it's your choice. Aside from the academic definitions of 'friend', it is important to understand that friendship, above all, is a relationship.

Whatever else may become of us when our leaf becomes withered and falls to the ground, we shall live on in the hearts of the people who share our love. I wish more people could have come to know people as I had, as friends when I was a child and throughout my life...

My Dad hired "Indians", as resort staff and to guide *tourists*, people who mostly came from the United States, to fish and hunt in Canada. These people, the "Indians" were different and amusing. In quiet conversation, they charmed us. They had an incredible, unscripted sense of humour. Masters, in the seemingly forgotten art of self-originated humour. Without radio, television, movies, or daily newspapers, they entertained themselves by using words, sounds, facial expressions and stories. They saw funny things around them that we didn't even notice. These people were, above all, my friends.

Personal differences are not an issue between friends. My friends made fun of themselves, each other, everything, and me. This including something as obscure as birds awkwardly landing on the branch of a tree. Never mean, their teasing had the precision of a good surgeon. Life was a constant ripple of giggles.

I see mankind, not above, but as a part of nature. Aboriginal teachings, unlike that of Euro/Religious teachings that tend to compartmentalize teachings and existence. I learned as a child never to debate the differences, but that was then...

Why do we call the descendants of the First Peoples of North America "Indians"? Did we do it because we could? Was it because we were the stronger and could get away with it?

The Canadian Constitution recognizes three groups of First Peoples – Indians, Métis, and Inuit. These are three separate peoples with unique heritages, languages, cultural practices and spiritual beliefs.

I prefer using "First People(s)[4] as opposed to "Indian" or First Nations, a term that came into common usage in the 1970s to replace "Indian". The term First Nation is to represent a governing body or governing standing

When he reached the Americas, it could not have taken Columbus more than a day or two to figure out that he wasn't in the suburbs of Bombay. The Europeans had been trudging off to India, using other routes, for centuries before Columbus set sail.

---

[4] Dr. Terri-Lynn Brennan – Community Engagement & Education Cultural Services, City of Kingston, Ontario Canada

We named places Bombay, Calcutta, Peking, and Siam. Now these places are Mumbai, Kolkata, Beijing, and Thailand. What happened? Did the West finally get a hearing aid? Did we have to change because China, India, and Thailand became more independent, more significant and stronger? Is the world coming to realize that we are all on the same planet and that maybe we might get along a little better if we could start listening to one another? Possibly so!

How did this happen? A little history: when Europeans first arrived in the Americas with their germs, their guns, and their religion, they found distinct peoples that they indiscriminately identified all as "Indians". The Spaniards killed and enslaved the people. The English and French created self-serving colonial military adversarial alliances to support competing Empire and economic expansion. After the War of 1812, it was deemed the time to end "Indian" friendships. Onetime friends were now obstructions to European colonial settlement and nation development.

Paul Martin said that; "Indigenous thought belongs in the classroom; furthermore, as Canadians, it is to ignore our origins as a nation at a time when the real need is to repair the consequences of those who treated this land a terra nullius, or a place where nobody lived, so many hundreds of years".

In 1867 Canada, "Indian" people were done a great injustice. Their children were taken from their homes and communities and put into Indian Residential Schools. Beginning in the 1870's, there came to be over 130 such schools located across Canada; the last of them closed in 1996. These schools were set up to eliminate parental involvement in the raising of their children. The intention was for the "Indian" population to assimilate into European-influenced Canadian society.

Is there any greater insult? Seven generations of people robbed of the joy parenthood, love of family and children. These are people forced by history's "well - meaning" tyranny to surrender their culture to the new way. As Phil Fontaine, Grand Chief of The Assembly of First Nations, said in May 2007, "We have a right to be frustrated, concerned, and angry".

Reconciliation and healing have begun, but we have not yet seen an end to "Indian" persecution and bigotry. We have a ways to go, but there is hope. First peoples are a dynamic, adaptive and enduring people: Their older cultural values continue to provide them with the order, satisfaction, identity and fullness of life.

I am not responsible for the failings of our forefathers, and the hurt caused to Canada's First Peoples. Colonialism is a part of our collective history, as were Indian Residential Schools only part of the process intended to assimilate and integrate Canada's Indigenous Peoples. What rose from this became widely accepted by a nation, and resulted in official programs (Laws) that to the public were thought positive and constructive. Is this not the "Perfect Crime"?

Relationship Building

My aim here is to share some very personal and honest reflections in the hope that people will embrace and build upon respectful relationship building. The time has come to step out from the past and begin to establish collaborative, inclusive community strategies.

People are stereotyping people, never stepping back from their cultural values far enough to understand why others may see the world differently. At the risk of generalizing, I would suggest that there exists a mindset, among some natural resource users and developers, which negatively portray the "Indian". The reaction is somewhat understandable of the disobedient actions of some in their search to have their long outstanding issues resolved. Both are wrong according to the counsel that I received from Elders, in my youth, who were irate over having a second-rate social status forced upon them.

Natural resources belong to no one but are here as a gift to all of creation. This concept is being overshadowed by protracted litigation, which is often guided by short-term interest and greed "what's-in-it-for-me" mentality.

There were two miscarriages justice: (1) Indian Reserves and (2) Indian Residential Schools forced First Peoples from being self-reliant social and economic independents to being dependencies. The remote geographic locations of many Indian Reserves have little or no sustainable future as a First Nation without having economic independence. Treaty promises will always remain tenuous, tied to the will and the ability of government and taxpayers. Individuals now face immense challenges with less than competitive educations, social and economic inclusion.

I can relate to First Peoples trying to assimilate into different social and economic environments. I remember my difficulties leaving the bush to live in Milwaukee, Wisconsin. My transition, though difficult, was pale compared to that of many First Peoples. My problem was no more than a teenager adjusting to a lifestyle that did not include fishing and hunting, but instead football, sports, and school. Unlike many First Nations children, I had empathetic parental and peer support to help me adjust.

First Nations and individuals continue to struggle with ongoing issues. I am convinced that all entities must commit to, and be accountable for, finding solutions to today's problems. Analyzing the past changes nothing, and projecting the future is often a way of avoiding dealing with the present.

Governments and First Nations quarrel about meetings, meeting agendas, and attendance, and engage in publicity antics, preposterous behavior, and witch-hunts. All the while, many of the First Peoples live in less than desirable conditions. Without social acceptance, financial independence, educational and employment opportunities, First Nation Communities are totally dependent upon federal funding, arms length bureaucracy, and decision-making. Many Chiefs and Councils struggle to allocate financial resources working from their underfunded program desks in the reality of day-to-day social crisis management.

Recent events have media attention, and mainstream Canadians have become aware of conditions existing in some of Canada's northern First Nation impoverished communities. Opinions and fault be as they may, it is unacceptable for people to be living, in what has been said to be Third World conditions in one the wealthiest countries in the world.

Undertaking a long-term resolve to the many grievances is complex, and there is no simple solution. I do, however, see three main issues.

First: Treaty obligations are understandable, considering the historic context of the Treaties, and the failure to define and honour them. The Canadian Federal Government has the mandated authority to decide Treaty issues and changes to existing federal legislation, i.e. The Indian Act. The British Crown relinquished all responsibility for Canadian domestic matters at the time of Confederation, including Treaties signed before and after 1867. Failure to accept this simple fact very often obstructs dealing with other important issues. Off-topic, "Treaty" talk creates frustration, impedes building trust relationships, and is a set up for false expectations and failure.

A brief mentioning of the importance of the "Treaty" is an appropriate way to open a meeting, but anything more becomes distracting rhetoric. Demonizing one another only leads to further ignorance, polarization, self-righteousness, and the seemingly never-ending litany of failure.

Second: We do not hear enough about what is working: First People cooperative partnerships between educators, industry, governments, and people of goodwill. It will take the collective wisdom to transform dysfunctional communities into self-reliant economically viable places of contentment and pride – places to live where tradition and self-determination prevail, which includes the challenge of attaining First Nation community stability. We must overcome administrative day-to-day crisis management. We live in a dynamic world, and the challenges included First Nation community stability.

We must define those matters that individuals have control over from those from which they do not. Media hype has brought attention to the plight of First Peoples. We should not tie the hands of those that we empower to negotiate legislative change – nation-to-nation policy and treaties. We cannot burden people with off-task issues and pointless interruption while we have a priority need to see progress on the long-standing Treaty and Indian Act issues.

Our citizen-based, parliamentary form of government, has, by design, empowered elected representatives to establish government policy and the law of the country. Also, we are members of the international community, and our treatment of Aboriginal people is being assessed on the world stage.

Third: There are misconceptions fostered by the fact that Canadians where not informed and have never learned, Aboriginal history. Many Canadians do not know the history of Indian residential schools, forced integration, and present-day circumstances. For some First People, self-determination is compounded by a less than competitive education, poverty, and

MILE POST 104 AND BEYOND

by the larger societies' misunderstanding and negative perception of "Native" people. In particular, urban residents struggle to re-establish a sense of self-identity and cultural values. To the puzzlement of some mainstream Canadians, many "Indians, Métis, and Inuit" struggle to remain living in, and intimate with, their cultural lands.

PHILLIP SAWDO CRIES

The absolute insanity of war

I am ten years old. Phillip Sawdo, who just came back from the war, works for my father. Phillip and I share the little cabin on the shore of Lake Windigoostigwan at our fishing lodge. Phillip drinks beer before going to bed. Phillip's jumping up in bed, deep breathing and his sobbing often awakens me. I ask him if he is all right. Phillip, in a startled voice, would say: "I am sorry to wake you up again, Bobby. I am having that bad dream again. It won't go away. It is about a bad thing that happened when I was in the war. You and I are the best of friends, and I ask you, please do not to tell anyone, not even your Mom and Dad about me having bad dreams. O.K.?" Until now, I have kept my promise to Phillip that long ago summer night in 1946. Phillip Sawdo cried, and this was why . . .

Phillip was my friend and boyhood hero. He treated me like a little brother. It was Phillip who taught me how to do things every country boy needs to know. Things like how to hand-roll cigarettes, split firewood, shooting positions and the safe way to carry my .22 calibre rifle and *poachers'* field craft. We talked endlessly about hunting, trapping, fishing and how to make and do things, but never directly about the war. I suspect that much of our talk about hunting had much to do with Phillip's father and his own military field craft training and combat experience.

MILE POST 104 AND BEYOND

Each morning we would get up together, and I would spend my days working alongside Phillip at whatever he was doing when he was not guiding American fishermen. Together we cut and piled wood, mixed gas for the outboard motors, fixed boats and canoes and cleared land. My dad had it made . . . two workers for the price of one. Dad never said anything about me smoking the *occasional* cigarette or using bad words so long as my mother didn't see or hear me. Dad said, "If a boy can work as a man he should be allowed to grow up and live like a man."

We never talked about the war or his bad dreams. That was until one evening after drinking several bottles of beer, Phillip began to sob and he took me in his arms and told me about the bad dream that would not go away. "Maybe if I tell you how awful it was for me and my guys having to kill so many young boys, not much older than you, I might get some peace."

During World War II, Philip had been a paratrooper in the Canadian Army. He was involved in many actions, including parachuting into France ahead of the Normandy invasion and jumping into Germany ahead of the Allied Forces crossing the Rhine River. Years later, his brother Robert told me that Phillip had seen and done it all.

Phillip tearfully told me his story: "Me and four other guys were sneaking our way alongside a road scouting Germans. Down the road there came marching one hundred Hitler Youth soldiers heading towards us, and our lines. We quickly took up a good defensive position and opened fire on them as they were passing by. They took cover behind a big stone fence at the bottom of a hill on the other side of the road. One of my guys knew to kill the boy carrying the mortar base plate that lay in the middle of the road. Without their mortar, they could not get at us. Also luckily for us, they had not been trained to fire a mortar by using a dead body as a baseplate. They did not know how to fire the weapon. We were protected from their rifle fire as we were well positioned behind piles of stone surrounded by the trees on the opposite side of the road."

"Looking through the scope on my sniper rifle, I could see that these German soldiers, who raised their heads above the stone fence to shoot at us, were scared young boys. We begged them, I begged them, and I begged them, Bobby, to put down their guns and walk up the hill and go home." He pounded the bed with his fist and said over and over again, "We could not make them understand to stop shooting at us and just go home. I did not want to kill them. I saw so much killing and didn't want to kill those little boys. I had to do it. I am so very sorry. I just wanted them to go home and be with their parents, but I had to kill them. I had to kill them. It was awful, and it won't go away." Phillip and I both cried. I still do!

"Instead of giving up the fight and going home they began sending out guys two or three at a time to retrieve the mortar base-plate. I killed most of them with my sniper rifle. The Hitler Youth soldiers had little training, and very little if any support from the Regular German army. They had been sent out alone to make trouble and to die. The last one, I shot, was their seventeen-year-old Hitler Youth lieutenant. All those scared little boys were dead. It was so awful, when it was over my guys cried, and I threw up. I am so sad for what I had to do that day, and it won't go away. I hope that the Great Spirit will someday forgive me so I can live in peace. Bobby, please don't tell anybody about this...." Dear Phillip, it is now time to tell your story. The absolute insanity of war!

Phillip had great physical strength and endurance. Now, in a more mature sense, Phillip was a testament to the demons he overcame. He found the strength to move on to have a full and rewarding life.

Phillip married Jean Tenniscoe and they raised a fine family of four boys and four girls. In North-western Ontario, he was a tourist operator, fishing and hunting guide, and fur trapper. I now know from his eldest son, Louis, that he kept his horrors-of-war to himself. Until now, his family never knew the real cause of his terrible nightmares.

Phillip Sawdo died in 1985 and rests alongside my father in the Atikokan cemetery. "Phillip, may your after-life journey be only to those places of beauty and everlasting peace. You live on in the hearts of the people who love you. Nitchie (Friend), *Bobby Wells*"

Footnote: Phillip Sawdo volunteered for Canadian Army active service on October 4, 1943 and received his discharge on April 8, 1946.

TRAPPER, BOB SAWDO

Storytelling, sitting around the evening campfire, is as synonymous with life in northern Canada as is flying from one lake to another in pontoon-equipped aeroplanes. The storytelling start-up that I like most is the Ottawa Valley colloquialism, "Mind the time when". Assemblages of men, with or without beverages, would in turn, tell retold tales of heroic feats of strength, stealth, skill, and survival as if they happened yesterday. In reality, many of the yarns were embellishments old enough to challenge living memory. Heroes of great-grandfather's day and the personal experiences of old men that had become legends in their minds were the essences of many an evening's entertainment. There were also stories told about people and events that did not need exaggeration. One such person was Phillip Sawdo's father, Mr. Bob Sawdo, a fur poacher renowned for his strength, endurance and his craftiness in evading Quetico Provincial Park Rangers. One such event is about an aeroplane crash so funny that to embellish it would be to spoil the very essence of the tale.

MILE POST 104 AND BEYOND

Mr. Bob Sawdo and his father came to Northwester Ontario from Escanaba, Michigan, in the early 1900's. They both had lost their jobs, which were hand [whip] - sawing white pine square ship timber. Steam-powered sawmills had replaced them. Mr. Sawdo was the strongest man I have ever known, and truly a legend of the extraordinary. I once saw him pick up a forty-five gallon drum of gasoline, lean over, and gently place the four hundred pound drum in a freighter canoe. At the time, he was in his mid-sixties.

Mr. Sawdo was as gentle and quiet as he was strong. He never boasted about himself, although he was unsurpassed by all the people who *unlawfully* trapped the Quetico Park. Mr. Sawdo was a respected friend of my father, who had been a park ranger for eleven years.

In 1946, Mr. Sawdo returned from a solo seven-week jaunt in the park, with thousands of dollars worth of contraband beaver pelts on his back. Late one December night my Dad opened the door. There, stood tired and hungry Mr. Sawdo, who said, "Good to see you Bobby, sorry to wake the family, but two Park Rangers put the chase to me at daybreak yesterday. They didn't get me or me fur". I have not forgotten this because it was the first time I had ever heard anyone call my dad "Bobby" to his face. "Jesus Christ Bob, you didn't bring your fur here did you?" "No, Bobby, I wouldn't do that. I've cached it far from your place. Don't worry Bobby, I will have it sold before those two young fellers ever gets here – that is, if they ever do."

Years later, park ranger, Dick Carnahan, told me that he and his partner didn't have a "hope-in-hell" of ever catching Sawdo; although the man was twice the age of these two strapping young war vets, and breaking trail on snowshoes with a near hundred pound pack on his back. Dick told me that when he and his partner, who gave pursuit at daybreak, stopped for their supper it was the same place Sawdo had stopped for his lunch. They then realized that this poacher could run faster scared than they could angry and broke off their chase. Mr. Sawdo began his escape from the Kawnipi Lake area in the Quetico Park some thirty-five air miles from sanctuary at my father's door.

Back then; people survived life in the bush by minding their own business and helping others, without question. Not to say that we did not entertain ourselves by making a joke of peoples' accents and behaviour that were different from our own. My mother allowed us our antics, as long as she considered that we were not gossiping or being malicious in the telling of our stories. We all did this. That was just the way it was!

LILLY'S PLANE CRASH

Remembered as the Funniest of all Plane Crashes

Lilly Nix, the daughter of Mr. Bob Sawdo, was, at the time of her near demise, a gentle middle-aged woman who spoke with a slight native accent. Separated from her husband for many years, Lilly had been cooking at her brother's fly-in-fishing lodge since late winter. By mid-August, 1957, Lilly was more than anxious to get out of the bush to spend a few days in town - Atikokan, Ontario.

Two weeks after her aeroplane ordeal she brought her story to me by travelling alone across thirty-five miles of Lac Des Milles Lacs in a small boat. She heard that I was alone at our lodge's island outpost camp doing repairs and had come to tell me of her big "fright".

Her tea half-finished, Lilly starts crying and laughing, at almost at the same time. She began telling me what had happened to her: "You know, Bobby, I was getting a little bushed being up there at Sanford Lake. I was there pretty near five months, and I wanted to go to town and buy myself some things and see a picture show."

"I got up early that morning, put on my good dress, and waited for that Nordstrom guy from Minneapolis, who had a camp on the lake, to come and get me with his little aeroplane. He was going home and promised to drop me off in Atikokan. He finally came, and I went down to the beach and got into his aeroplane. He helped me tie the belt that holds you in your seat when you ride in an aeroplane. You know, Bobby, dat belt is damn dangerous."

"After Nordstrom had me tied in his aeroplane, he went to pull on that propeller. When the engine started, he turned the plane around so that the front pointed down the lake. I sit for a while then I get worried sitting there alone, and I lean over to look, and dat were when it happened. The aeroplane engine made a big noise making the propeller spin very fast. I think that when l lean over to look for Nordstrom, my big tit push in the red nob. That was the start of my big scare."

The further Lilly got along with her story the more she would break into tears, laugh, or do both at the same time. Thankfully, I could contain my laughter.

Lilly said, "I look again, and Nordstrom is standing on da beach waving his arms and there me is going down the lake, and I don't know how to drive an aeroplane. The further down the lake I go the faster I go. I think, I had better get the hell out. I had a hell-of-time to make loose the belt and to get myself out that little door. You know Bobby, I am pretty big."

"I got myself out the door and onto one of the canoes just in time because that goddamn aeroplane was about to jump off the water and fly with nobody driving it. I jump off. You know Bobby, if you jump off one of those dam tings don't jump between the canoes. I did, and my hair get catch on some wires and I think I will drown when my hair pull out. Goddamn that hurt. The aeroplane jumps off the lake and flies crooked crashing into the jack pine trees on the side of the hill."

"There I am, away out in the lake, with a sore head, wearing my good dress. Thank God I can swim. I swim back to the beach and when I get close Nordstrom start throwing rocks at me and calling me a goddamn Indian. To get away from that blasted fool, I swim out around the point to get out of the lake. Was I ever tired and damn mad too. That bastard is some lucky I didn't have a gun with me that day. My head, where my hair got pulled out, still hurts."

It took Lilly well over two hours to tell her story. There were many pauses, crying, laughing and her just sitting quiet. Lilly finally said, "I just had to come to you with this Bobby because I know you will tell people about the bad thing that happened to me. You know Bobby; a person could get killed in one of those goddamn things or even worse, *get hurt*."

I have told Lilly's story many times over the years, but this is the first time I have ever attempted to write it. Lilly lived three miles down the railroad track from our lodge and treated me as a loving aunt when I was child. Lilly passed a long time ago and as humorous as I think her aeroplane story I remember Lilly most, as a loving, faithful friend.

LIVING THE BUSH LIFE

1960 – 1965

People that live in Canada's vast wilderness, the 'bush', are a colourful thread in the tapestry of Canadian history. What follows are personal experiences reminiscent of our life, very different than how we live today.

Our Lac Des Mille Lacs Trapline:

In 1960, my father sold the Wells' Fishing Lodge. I moved with my husky dog team to a recently purchased Registered Trapline located on Lac Des Mille Lacs, thirty-six miles from the town of Upsala.

In January, Inge, my fiancée, became my trapping partner and soul mate. We spent the winter in a log cabin that was big enough for an army cot, table, stove and two chairs. Our four dogs were kept outdoors tied to trees. We were isolated many miles from the nearest human being; *but we were close.*

MILE POST 104 AND BEYOND

Suzie

In our early years, transportation was four husky dogs. We functioned well together. Suzie, the team's lead-dog, taught us the importance of having different relationships with each dog. Wolf pack culture is not a democracy.

With the exception of Suzie, the other dogs, kept tied to trees, were not to come indoors. Suzie wanted outside within five minutes. It was too warm in the cabin for her. Because she was the respected leader of the team, she was always fed first. Suzie allowed us to pet her while she ate, while the others did not.

One early winter day, shortly after the lakes froze, I broke through the ice while working beside a beaver house. Instinctively, I called "Suzie". In an instant, she freed herself from her harness, carefully climbed down the side of the ice-slippery beaver house, and extended her head so that I could grab hold of her collar. The look in her eyes told me, "Leave the pulling to me and don't pull me into the water". Days earlier, she growled at me when I was about to attach her neck collar to dog the sleigh harness. If I had, she would not have been able to come to my rescue. Dogs tell you immediately if they like or do not like something.

Inge did several miles on snowshoes every two weeks for mail and small supplies. Our only other contact with civilization was Inge's battery-operated radio. The Thunder Bay radio station, CKPR, provided programming that linked people living in the bush without a telephone or two-way communications. Her radio, and an occasional aeroplane overhead, made us feel connected to the outside world.

There was an occasion when our bed became overcrowded. Inge had gone back to bed without first coming outside to pet and play with the dogs, when being harnessed to the toboggan for our daily Trapline run of 15 to 20 miles. I turned my back for a moment, and our well-disciplined team were in the cabin, fighting each other for room on the bed as they tried to dig Inge out from the Woods' Five Star sleeping bag. Getting our four furry friends outside and settled down was a challenge. To complicate the extraction was the nine-foot toboggan they pulled inside the cabin. From then on, although the temperature might be minus 40 degrees, Inge got dressed and came outside to pet and play with the team, as I harnessed them.

The last mile of our return home each afternoon was the ultimate of excitement. Inge, expecting us to round the point, would be standing out on the ice. When the dogs saw her, I had best be on the toboggan or be left to walk. It did not matter how hard our day had been, the team always reserved energy for their top speed one-mile run for home. There was a special bond between us.

When that trapping season ended, we bought a small housetrailer and truck, got married, and moved to Kyro's 1,000 Island Resort. Though still very much in the bush, we no longer traveled by dog team for supplies and the mail.

From an early age, my father and Aboriginal friends taught me survival skills, self-reliance, and the importance of your choice of

MILE POST 104 AND BEYOND

partner. Inge was my partner; she adapted quickly from urban to bush life. I told her many times that she was my very best trapping partner. I ran the Trapline and did the skinning. Inge stretched and dried the pelts, mostly beaver. It took approximately 78 nails to nail a beaver pelt on a drying board. The perfect partner! She also did all the cooking!

Beaver pelts Inge nailed to a stretching board and put outdoors to "Frost Dry"

OUR WEDDING DAY

April 29. 1961

Inge, Bridesmaid Laurie Reed[5] & Bob

There are many jokes made, and songs sung, about the bridegroom being left waiting on the church steps. It happened to me. Keeping to the marriage conventions of the day, Inge and I travelled in separate vehicles to the little white church in Upsala, Ontario. When I left for church, the twenty-mile gravel road had retained enough night frost to support the truck. Inge's departure was one hour later. By then the April morning sun had thawed the road in many places. Three times on her way to the church they

---

[5] **Laurie Reed was one of the many Murdered (Winnipeg) Aboriginal Women of the 1970s'.**

became stuck up to the car's rocker panels in mud. Everyone had to get out, except hopefully my bride-to-be, jack up the car, put planks under the wheels, and push...

My bride, in her spotless wedding dress and high-heeled shoes, arrived at the church two hours late. How was this possible? Prudently, she had put her knee-high rubber boots in the car before departing.

George Edwards' Wedding Day Teaching: George's father had been a Hudson Bay Factor and fur buyer at Savanne, Ontario, and his mother was from the Lac Des Mille Lacs Indian Reserve. George, at the time, was in his late 50's and had been a good friend of my family and me for many years. George once told me that, "I walk with a moccasin on one foot and a boot on the other–both are good". He took me aside the day Inge, and I got married:

- "Do not walk in front of your wife, as she may not follow. Do not walk behind your wife, as you may not be lead. Walk beside each other as friends, except when she carries the canoe you walk ahead with the gun. My mother told me that in time I would come to understand the meaning of these words. I seem not to have as my wife went another way. I think that you are a pretty smart guy Bob, and I hope you understand."

Inge and I have been together for more than fifty years.

HOME AND FAMILY

We lived at Kyro's 1,000 Lakes Resort where Inge worked summers as a dining room waitress while I guided fishermen on Lac Des Mille Lacs. In the autumn I guided moose hunters. In the summer we lived in an eight by twenty-eight foot trailer. For the winter we would move across the road into a small four-room cabin. Winter life at the resort was quite different than in the summer. The people had now gone for the winter and our running water and diesel generated electricity also "left" with them.

Our first move to winter quarters I recall as being both awful and wonderful – one of the memorable days. Inge wasn't there to help with the packing and carrying of our belongings from the trailer to the winter cabin. I had to do it all myself in the two hours before driving to Thunder Bay to pick up Inge and our newborn son, Perry, from the hospital. Inge's one hundred mile ride home was not made easier or faster by a blinding snow and sleet storm. Arriving home from the whole experience, she opened the door to a room filled with boxes and stuff scattered everywhere. Thankfully, two women from the resort had come in and made ready the bed and fixed the place up a little before they departed from the resort for the winter. I had flown home the night before from ten days of guiding moose hunters. Our baby Perry was at home. It didn't seem as bad as it had when we first opened the door. We were together – how much more wonderful can it be?

Perry, whose outdoor play language was Anishinabek, until the age of four, retired from the Canadian Army in 2015 as a Lieutenant-Colonel.

OUR FIRST SNOWMOBILE

Inge riding our 1962 Olympic Ski Doo

We were the first to have a Ski Doo snowmobile in the Upsala area. People drove for miles to look and stand around, voicing their opinions about this new-fangled thing. New-fangled, maybe, I now got home most every night. Fur production and income increased, as did the amount of time Inge spent nailing beaver pelts to stretching-boards.

Annually, we would harvest about two hundred beaver, fifty mink, and a dozen otter. Pelt-preparation took place in our kitchen. I did most of the skinning and Inge stretched, dried, and removed the pelts from the stretcher-boards, with the help of our two-year-old son Perry. When it was minus twenty degrees outside, the pelts would be put outside to frost dry.

MILE POST 104 AND BEYOND

We put in long days preparing our catch for sale to the Hudson Bay Company in Thunder Bay. Fortunately, Perry was able to sleep through all the noise of Inge nailing beaver pelts to the stretching-boards.

DO YOU HAVE RUNNING WATER IN THE WINTER?

Bob – Two pails 'running' through the deep snow

Summer guests at the lodge, interested in our winter life, would often ask Inge if she had running water in the winter. She would jokingly show them my photograph carrying two pails of water – "my running water". Inge now admits that having to carry water was awful because she would have to leave the baby alone in the cabin. Going for water involved having to negotiate a snowed-over path to the lake, cutting open the frozen water hole, and carrying two pails of water, without spilling them, back to the cabin. When I was away she had to make three trips daily to wash baby diapers. The challenge was not only having water to wash baby diapers but also hanging them out to dry. It got very cold in January and February, as were Inge's fingers when hanging wash on the clothesline. There were days when the clothesline would be completely buried in snow. Potty training took on a new degree of urgency.

PUTTING SOME BALANCE IN OUR LIVES

The belief that I was adaptable to nature was what attracted me to the life as a trapper. Living in harmony with nature is not always easy on a day-to-day basis. Few people could tolerate such a solitary existence, and there was no need for us to do so. We had road access to the Trans-Canada-Highway though not always drivable, so we were not completely cut off from civilization.

Winter driving takes on a different meaning when you live where we did. We never left for Thunder Bay without first packing a Woods' Five Star Eiderdown sleeping bag, additional warm clothes, emergency food, shovel, and axe in our vehicle. Some winter nights, when driving home from Thunder Bay, we would drive fifty-mile stretches without seeing another car or truck. Trips to the city were when there was no snow in the forecast.

Inge was my perfect partner and excellent Mommy. Without modern conveniences, she prepared meals, found time to read, knit, and do needlework. I'd come home to find a clothesline full of wash, chores done, and my dinner being served by my wife, looking as if she had spent the day at the spa.

Winter parkas and felt boots are great, but so are dresses and 'red' high-heeled shoes. Once each month, we would go to Thunder Bay, to sell our fur and to resupply. Though these were working outings, we always looked forward to a day in 'town'. Each New Year's Eve was spent in Thunder Bay. Leaving Perry with a babysitter in our hotel room, all "dressed up," we would join in the celebrations downstairs. There were occasions when Inge would leave Perry with me and go to the city and spend her day trying on shoes, hats, and going to flower and fabric stores. She said, "It was wonderful to get out of the bush for a day but more wonderful to get back home."

FRIENDS & NEIGHBOURS

Inge soon came to appreciate the Chicago and Peters families, our only winter neighbours. It was her first close association with people living the traditional Ojibwa culture, a way of life that was much different from where she had come from, Germany. It appeared to her that these people had an unregimented lifestyle of non-interference, without any authority figures telling them what and when to do things. Most incredible for her, was that these people respected people's differences, and their willingness to help in ways never before imagined. For example:

One morning Chief Tom Peters knocked on our door, most unusual, as he would never come to our cabin when I was not at home. Tom told Inge that she was about to run out of fuel oil. Inge said the tank had just been filled; he said, "Tank empty". Then he turned around and walked seventeen miles out to the highway and telephoned the oil company, and then he walked back to tell Inge the truck was coming. Tom and his family lived a half mile across the lake. Seeing the difference in the smoke coming out of our chimney, Tom could tell that we would soon be out of oil. The truck that had delivered us fuel oil a week earlier had only partially filled our tank. When I got home, I thanked Tom, who said, "Oh that's nothing – your family are neighbours and our friends and would do the same for us." So true! After this, we always had forty-five gallon drums of fuel oil and working oil stove in reserve.

The Chicago Family

The Chicago family lived across the road from us. Mrs. Frances Chicago took the best of care of Perry while Inge was at work. Whenever he needed changing, or his clothes got the least bit soiled, on went a new set of clean clothes. Thankfully, Inge did not have to hand-wash clothes in the summer as she did in the winter. She was said to be the resort's best Laundromat customer, thanks to Frances. As Perry was learning to speak English from us, by playing with Frances' three little children, he also learned the Anisanabic language. He would never speak it when at home or in our presence. I'm sure Frances told him never to let your parents hear you talking "Indian", or they won't let you come here anymore. How wrong she was! Whenever one of her children or Perry would see us, their usual chatter stopped.

Frances Chicago & ten month old Perry

The Chicago family did not cut firewood in preparation for winter. Instead, each afternoon George Chicago would come outside, look at the sky and go back inside. Moments later, his wife Frances and their three children would head off down the trail with a sleigh, saw, and axe to cut firewood. Each day they would return with varying amounts of wood as determined by George's weather prediction. Needless to say, he didn't always get it right. When George got it wrong, Frances and the kids would leave in the dark the following morning to go and cut wood.

Inge never quite understood why. I have heard two explanations: The first is that Native people are lazy; the second is, if they were to cut and pile wood outside, others will come and take it. This act is not considered "stealing" in traditional native communities of the north. I do not believe either to be true. My Elder Teachings' are the long-forgotten wisdom; meant to survive the winter doldrums. This daily activity gets the people outside of their traditionally small, overcrowded winter quarters when there would be no reason to go outside. Please, take a moment and place yourself in a sixteen by twenty foot cabin with six other people, with no radio, television, or books. Aboriginal Peoples survived thousands of years in the Canadian north – not by being lazy.

I asked George why he pretended that he could not understand or speak English. George may not have been the most ambitious fox in the forest, but I think he just may have been the smartest. He told me that it is easier not to understand English than to spend all day answering fishermen's questions about what it is like to be an "Indian". And, when people wanted him to do things that he did not want to do, it was fun for him to watch their antics and frustration trying to make him understand what they wanted him to do. And, to watch them doing it themselves, trying not to laugh and to look bewildered.

George would take me aside for a laugh about his 'dumb "Indian" act of the day'. I would tell George, "Do not spoil your play by getting drunk, and all of a sudden be able to speak English." "George", I said once to him, "don't drink whiskey and talk English. Just drink whiskey". His reply was, "O.K."

The Peters Family

Chief Tom and his wife had a daughter that everyone called Princess. I came home one day from visiting Tom and couldn't wait to tell what I had just seen. Apparently it was Princess' job each afternoon to bring in the firewood for the night. She made this into her afternoon play. First she would harness a husky dog to a toboggan and then put her cat, yes, cat, in similar type harness and attach it also to a little sleigh her father had built. The threesome would go single file, Princess, dog and cat, to the woodshed a short distance away. Princess loaded the dog's toboggan with the firewood for the night and the cat's sleigh with kindling for starting the morning fire. I couldn't believe my eyes seeing that a cat could be trained to do anything, let alone learn to be harnessed like a dog and pull a sleigh. There is more!

I apparently showed a little too much interest in Princess' wood hauling, which she interpreted as me having a romantic interest in her. Well, after her parents had gone to bed, Princess knocked on our door, came inside, sat down, and made loving eyes at me. She spoke very little if any English but she never spoke a word for over two hours. Sometime well after midnight we ran out of hospitality, we helped her on with her parka, escorted her to the door, bid her goodnight, closed and bolted the door behind her. Princess was in her late teens, very much overweight and only got away from home when she would run away. I swear to this day, that whenever I saw her coming, I turned and ran the other way.

JACK'S SECRETS AND DREAMS

Perry the time has come to tell you Jack Ogama's secret.

Perry James Wells
Bosnia 1996

Jack Ogama was well over six and a half feet tall and weighed more than three hundred pounds. He and his wife would be flown out to their trap line each fall and back to the Resort in the spring.

MILE POST 104 AND BEYOND

Their winter life in the bush was a gentle interface with nature and without contact with the modern world. Their only food purchased would be tea, flour, baking powder, salt, lard, sugar, and special dog food for their little dog. Everything else, they hunted, fished, or gathered. Once each winter, Jack would snowshoe the thirty miles out of the bush to sell his fur and to buy a few treats for his wife and dog.

One spring, I drove them to Port Arthur (Thunder Bay) for Mrs. Ogama to have a badly infected tooth extracted. It was the first time in over 20 years that they had been to the city. Terrified by the traffic all three of us would have to hold hands when crossing the street. Completely fascinated by an escalator we had to have repeated rides before being allowed to carry on to the dentist.

Inge often asked: "What do the two of you talk about?" My only reply was "Jack's secrets and dreams." Jack asked that I tell his "secrets and dreams" long after he and his wife entered the spirit world. I wish I could mimic Jack's voice as we sat visiting outside most evenings, swatting mosquitoes, and smoking "tailor-made" cigarettes, as I waited for Inge to come home from work.

Jack Ogama told me his family had come from the United States. "I tell the people here, including my wife, that I am Ojibway and maybe a little Cree. I talk the same way they do, but my people are not Ojibway, they are Lakota [The Lakota people are part of a confederation of seven related tribes of the Sioux Nation]. I can no longer talk the Lakota way for I have not heard it spoken for a very long time. When I was a little boy, my Grandfather told me about the time my people came to live in Canada. Many white soldiers riding big horses were chasing them from their territory in the United States. The Queen said she would keep my people safe. The American soldiers say we did a bad thing. A long time ago many of my people and other Indian warriors killed all the soldiers and their chief with the long blond hair. The grandmothers poked holes with sticks in the ears of that longhaired soldier so that in his next life he would hear better. He was a bad man and would not listen to my people, and that is why they had to kill him."

"White soldiers and many white people came to take the gold from our land. They did a bad thing to the land, and they were also very bad to my people. It was a very good day for our warriors. My grandfather was a boy warrior. He rode a horse and had his own gun in the big fight. The Big Chief gave him a special feather because he was very brave and fought without fear. When I asked if he had killed many soldiers, he would say nothing, turn his head, and look to the ground. A long time ago they buried the special feather with my grandfather."

"This big fight made the white soldiers very mad, and my people had to run away like dogs. I have never before told anyone this story about my people and me, not even my wife. I have been afraid that the grandchildren of the soldiers will come and kill me because my people killed the long-hair soldier and his warriors, who wore blue coats and rode big horses that we took."

I was amazed that Jack did not know that his grandfather told of the 1876 Battle of the Little Bighorn and that the 'long-hair' soldier he talked about was United States General George Armstrong Custer.

"I don't know if this was a bad thing my people did. My grandfather said it was a good thing to kill the soldiers. What do you think, Bob? I tell you my secret, Bob, because you are the only white man that has ever been my friend or person I truly trust. I know that you will keep my secret until a long time after I die. Someday, a long time after I die, you must tell my big secret to your boy and other people so my spirit can be free. You must wait and become old yourself before you tell my secret to Quezance [boy] because young people must have a trouble free spirit for them to make a good path in their life while on earth."

"Holy Men are different because the Creator has given them the power to become strong from the troubles of others. If they are not Holy Men, their eyes will become dim and they will not see all the good things that the Creator has given. You too, Bob, should not think about these things now because your journey is still young. After I die, my spirit can wait to be set free. I do not like people to take my picture because my spirit might get trapped on a piece of paper, and I thank you for telling American tourists not to take my picture."

Jack also shared one other secret. Over a lifetime, he had saved a great deal of money, not because he ever intended to spend it, nor did he fully understand its value, but he saved his money because he wanted to. He showed me his money, saved from over thirty years of working summers and winter trapping. His traditional lifestyle required very little money. His one exception was summers at the Resort, when he bought many Pepsi and T-bone steaks. He kept his money, including a two-inch stack of one hundred dollar bills, in two canvas bags hung around his neck. He asked me that if anyone ever stole his money would I help him find and kill the bad person – God forbid! Fortunately, no one ever did.

Jack also told me about his recurring dream that first came to him after he saw a frog with five legs. In his dream, a loon and a pileated woodpecker came to tell him that the Manitou God Spirit and the Windigo Devil Spirit were both very angry at what the white man was doing to nature. They cut down all the trees; there is nowhere for the birds and animals to live. They put bad things in the water that killed the fish and too much bad smoke in the air making it smell wrong.

"The woodpecker and loon said that Manitou and Windigo are searching for a peacemaker spirit. They want to come together and make their great powers into one so as to be wise and strong enough and make all these bad things stop. All people must stop fighting with nature, or much bad will come. Maybe when I die, my spirit will become the peacemaker so this can happen. You think that is a good idea, Bob"? I did then and do now, think it is a good idea.

As a family, we met to say goodbye for the last time knowing we would not see each other again. Jack picked up our four-year-old son, Perry, with his huge hands. He held him close and told him in the Ojibway/Anishinabek language, "Quezance (boy) your Daddy will some day tell you my big secret, go, grow up to become a soldier-warrior and fight for the good of the people and our land." Before putting Perry down, he first blew his breath on his forehead each time before he held him outright. First in the direction of the east, then the south, west and north each time saying, "Quezance take the spirit of a Warrior".

Except for his enormous size, Jack Ogama was mostly disregarded being ethnically and culturally different. However, this did not stop us from being the very best of friends. Jack told me his innermost thoughts, his dreams. He had grave concerns about what the Omchagochi (white man) was doing to our home.

As a boy, I learned from Native Elder teachings that they had spiritual beliefs that were different from my Christian teachings. Jack explained that when he died his spirit would not go to a destination like heaven or hell but on an unknown journey. His afterlife journey may be alone in a blinding snowstorm without feelings, or it may be one that takes into account all the good things from his life. Unfortunately, he could not prepare for his afterlife journey, as there were no Holy Men, to help him see past today. He worried about himself and the many "Indian" people who had lost their way with the spirits. Also, there was no one who would pray for him and others, so that their afterlife journey would be a good one.

Without imposing, Jack asked if I would pray for his spirit when he died. He said that I could pray to my God or Manitou, as it would make no difference. His wife told him to tell me that, "The white man's God and the Manitou were one of the same, the Creator, only that we see through different eyes". Jack was very saddened that there were no Holy Men in this area that he could ask to pray for him, and the other native people who he worried would become lost in their afterlife. "It is too bad but many native people in this area no longer pray to the spirits in the old ways. The spirits are very sad."

"Bob, you and I will see each other again. I will go first and find a nice place beside a lake, without mosquitoes, where we can make a shore lunch. We will smoke tailor-made cigarettes, drink tea with sugar and talk about trapping, going hunting and catching big fish. Maybe you will tell me where the good places are to fish like you do now – you are my friend – you are my Brother."

THROWN TO THE BEAR

Why, having been twenty feet off the ground for eight hours hunting from a climbing-tree stand, would bring to mind an adventure fifty-year past, is beyond me. It may have had to do with brain overload or some other malfunction. At the time, I was judiciously trying to become disengaged from a Gatorade bottle. As this is not the story, we shall move along.

What happened back then may not fit the true definition of a hunt, but the adventure had all the necessary criteria of a memorable hunt, such as the out-of-doors, the north woods, wildlife, a firearm, partnership, the totally unexpected, and an event worthy of memory. At the time, Inge and I worked, (she as

MILE POST 104 AND BEYOND

a waitress and I as fishing and hunting guide) at Kyro's Thousand Lakes Resort on Lac Des Mille Lacs near Upsala, Ontario.

It began, at first light, one August day, with words every married man has heard, disturbing his intimate dreams, "I hear something". No doubt about it! Large clawed paws, six inches from my head, were looking for a grip, trying to rip the aluminum skin off the end of the twenty-eight foot wheeled hallway we affectionately called our summer home.

Sitting up, I pulled aside the curtain and pressed my nose against the window going eyeball to eyeball with a 150 pound, cross-eyed black bear who also had his nose pressed to the same spot, on the other side of the window. Seeing this, Inge went into action as only she can do. In a single movement, she jumped from the bed and shoved my 'go-to' model 94 Winchester at me. In pre-9/11 times, self-reliant country people did not have to search for gunlock keys and ammunition. We kept a gun at the ready, to defend the cave and to put passing game on the dinner table. Believe me, I was also willing to take *"Bear"* action, but first I had a Fruit-of-the-Loom containment problem. Inge did not think this to be very important just then, and so I found myself, rifle-in-hand, in the open doorway. As they say, behind every good man stands a good woman. Inge was there.

Seeing the bear in the back of our half-ton pickup, parked six meters away, presented a rare opportunity. "Drop the varmint in his tracks, already loaded for burial transport." But, just as I was about to squeeze the trigger, he jumped from the back of the truck straight at us standing in the doorway. Simultaneously, Inge's maternal instincts kicked-in and with two firm and forceful hands she gave me one mighty shove. The door slammed shut, as I belly flopped in the mud at the same time as that cross-eyed bear hit the ground. Again, face-to-face, less than two meters apart crouched the most scared bear that I have ever seen. Somehow, while still lying flat on my face on the rain soaked lawn, I fired off a shot that dropped him as he was about to round the end of the trailer.

Inge was both crying and laughing at the same time, with two-year old son Perry in her arms. "Did you get him?" she asked. Seeing my reflection in the full-length mirror, butt naked, rifle in hand and covered in dirt, I said, "He looks dead. Thanks to your quick thinking. He died from fright". Me, scared? Hell no! I just don't like being thrown to the bears without my running shoes on. Laughter replaced all hint of tears.

However, our final laugh of the day came that evening as we were gathered as a family to bury the bear. Perry asked, "Daddy, why are you burying your underwear?"

Still Smiling 50th Wedding Anniversary 2011
Inge and Bob Wells

TIME TO MOVE ON

It was time to gather up the experiences of my nine-year adventures and to move on. Soon we should need a school for Perry. For a long time, it had been my dream to become a conservation officer and the encouragement from conservation officer friends helped Inge and me to move on. Although I knew the client groups of the job - the tourist industry, fishermen, hunters, trappers and, yes, the poachers well, I first needed to go back to school. After attending the Ontario Forest Technical School in Dorset, Ontario for one year I became a Conservation Officer and had a twenty-eight year career with the Ontario Department of Lands and Forests/Ministry of Natural Resources.

"TOWER MAN" – INGE WELLS

1966 - 1970

Seven days a week, Inge left the house mornings with her lunch in-hand, walked up the hill and climbed the one-hundred-foot fire tower, where she spent up to ten hours searching for smoke. Spotting smoke, she would radio her compass bearing which combined with those of others provided an accurate location to dispatch fire-fighting crews.

One afternoon, two male American tourists, in their early thirties, climbed the tower. On opening the trapdoor they looked in at her wearing only a bathing suit, and asked if she was the "tower man". She said, "Have another look"!

I would be remiss not to mention the unpaid women of the Department of Lands and Forests (Ontario Ministry of Natural Resources). Women, with rare exception, were the wives of staff. Until the 1980's, most staff working in the north lived on Government Bases. Single men lived in staff houses and married men in government-provided single-dwelling homes.

Women, who were waged, mostly filled clerical positions in our early years. My wife Inge was an exception. She was one of the first female Fire Tower observers in Ontario. From 1966 to 1970, she was known as "Upsala Tower". Fire Towers and aircraft patrol were Ontario's Forest Fire Detection System. Towers were located to give overlapping fields of view so as to triangulate smoke sighting, critical for fast response fire suppression. There were times when people remained in the towers when thunderstorms approached. They recorded lightning strikes and then watched for smoke that may show up any time over a period of several days. This practice ended when Inge's fire tower neighbour, Mr. Koko Kuie at the Raith fire tower, was hit by lightning, blowing the sides off his tower cabin. Badly shaken, Mr. Koko Kuie escaped injury. A few days off (without pay), aided by liquid medicating, saw Koko back to work in a new tower cabin.

John Bouchard once looked out of his tower window to see a jet fighter fly past at eye level. He swears that the pilot had blue eyes. The next day, John could be seen hanging out the window on a rope, painting the tower cabin orange. As he said, "Orange was a colour easier seen on foggy days by low flying aeroplanes".

Inge's unofficial position was wife of the conservation officer. Most Conservation officer's wives took phone messages, and would "lie to people asking where the game warden was patrolling".

One-day, dinner was not forthcoming. I had locked the deep freezer filled with seized game and fish. Continuity of evidence or not, she got a key. Thirty-five years later, I am still reminded of the times when I called her into service at 3:30 A.M. to prepare meals for a bunch of officers and myself, working nights.

Wives were not the only ones called upon for help. My teenaged son Perry, riding our personal snowmobile, accompanied me on twenty-five to fifty mile weekend patrols, in the event my issued machine broke down. In other words, we did my job as a family.

This unofficial family support was, in turn, give-and-take. For example, one year I had an assignment that kept me from home the week before Christmas. The Chief Ranger sent a vehicle to take Inge and Perry into North Bay and back for last minute Christmas shopping. At an earlier posting, one hundred miles from the district office, my supervisor told me that he wanted to see me at the district office not less than once a month. He said, "Bring your family when you come to town as I'm sure they would enjoy a day out of the bush."

A CONSERVATION OFFICER LOOKS BACK

Bob & Skipper 1968

Conservation Officer responsibility for the enforcement and management of fish and wildlife in rural Ontario was my dream job. Dealing with my daily priorities, I made a joke of far off theoretical based strategic and operational planning done at higher-level far off offices. My priority of the day was very often decided by a late night, at home, phone call reporting poaching, an animal kill, or some person in need of help. There were also days that I'd drive to the end of the driveway before deciding whether to turn right or left, but always with a purpose in mind. I went to bed anxious for morning so I could get back at it again.

My upbringing of fishing, hunting, trapping, and guiding provided valuable experiences for me as a Conservation Officer. Knowing the client groups made my conversation, assistance, and the apprehending of poachers relatively easy. My years as a field officer were at a time when Conservation Officers patrolled mostly alone, without reliable radio communication, dependent on help from the (love/hate) community, and the Provincial Police. On several occasions, my wife would be called upon to pick me up, in our personal vehicle, at the end of my night canoe patrol for poachers spearing fish. Seized fish, were donated to seniors' centers and local people in need.

I was close to the natural resources I loved, and had the opportunity to learn from people trained in the sciences of resource management. Early in my career, I found myself part of a transition. University-trained resource managers were beginning to seek counsel from people like my father; people who lacked formal education, but had years of life learning. I encouraged young graduates to put away their book-learned and go learn from the Elders who had walked the ground and paddled the rivers of time. Make the time for conversation and listening. There was a time, if, it wasn't in the book then it was considered "folklore". Am I now hearing the rhymes of history trying to repeat itself?

When my family and I commenced my Conservation Officer career in 1966, we became members of a large corporate culture. 'We are a family doing good for natural resources, here to help each other, and the people of our community. If a job needed doing the people rallied to assist. Mandated staff and assets were often called upon to help in areas outside of our responsibilities. I once got the nod from my supervisor to detail staff to dig a grave in the community cemetery for a lady who had passed away. The 'forestry' as it was often called back then, routinely provided air and ground transport for medical or other emergencies. Dedicated medical transport had not reached Ontario's north. It was not uncommon to see a 'Forestry' Lands and Forests truck dumping a load of firewood logs in a senior's front yard instead of leaving them in the woods to rot. We thought of this as a public service.

By the time I retired in 1993, it was common to hear mid-level resource managers contemplating the will of the 'political masters' when coming to resource management decisions. Staff had become disgruntled at not being able to do their jobs. They came to the realization that the organization they once loved, no longer loved them back. Decisions, once made standing beside my truck, had been moved into the political jungle, which caused considerable gridlock. There were large cuts in staff and operational funding, resulting in program cuts and identity loss.

These same 'political masters' have also muzzled our professional resource and environment managers from speaking freely to the media for fear they may say something politically incorrect, or worse, politically damning. Instead, communications get vetted through politically responsive communication people more concerned with appearance than the actual issues.

There was a time when professional natural resource and environmental staff publically debated resource and environmental issues...

WHY DID THE COYOTES MOVE TO TOWN?

The winter of 2010 was not the first nor will it be the last time that urbanites awaken to the fact that wildlife exists elsewhere than on television. Coyotes have taken up residence in towns and cities. Letters to the Editor express outrage over the mysterious disappearance of cats and small dogs. The coyote situation had become horrifying —"children may no longer be safe as they wait for the school bus". Social gatherings had the usual round of opinions about what they, whoever they may be, must do to make neighbourhoods safe — reinstate the wolf and coyote bounty — do something...

I include this topic as an example of how far many have become removed from the reality that nature is dynamic. Wildlife populations are on constant increases and declines. 2010 urban increases in the coyote population were mostly the result of previous winter mortality of overpopulated deer herds. The disappearance of the large deer population in the woods caused the corresponding large coyote population to go elsewhere in search of a meal — to town.

I write, "The Coyote Speaks" in an attempt to bring some sense of reality to wildlife dynamics. The urban coyote population will decline for a few years but will return when the forces of nature have their way.

The Coyote Speaks – "What do you know about me?"

"I am not surprised that many of you are again determined to wage a vicious war against my kind and me. Ever since white settlers arrived, with the view that we coyotes are a bloodthirsty lot of killers with no redeeming qualities, we have mostly been persecuted. It hasn't always been this way. My ancestors lived for centuries alongside native North Americans with little conflict. Those people appreciated us as fellow creatures, told admiring stories about our cleverness and called us Tricksters. But, of course, those people saw themselves as a part of nature. They may have also known that, above all else, we coyotes were survivors.

Not many animals have been able to hold their own against the forces of civilization. We have prevailed, and I will tell you how: In ancient times, our mortal enemies, the wolves, forced coyotes to live in areas where no one type of food was plentiful or always available. But unlike wolves, who have a complex social structure and hunt large animals in packs, we coyotes have a more arduous situation and survive as opportunists. Although we kill deer, we are more likely blamed for killing a deer that has died of other causes. We are not fussy eaters, and we can survive on fruit, grain, frogs and toads, birds, mice, rabbits, and other small creatures, including the occasional cat or small dog. We make no distinction between natural and unnatural food, including your garbage. A meal is a meal!

We usually scavenge and hunt alone. We will enlist the assistance from family members in the winter to protect carrion from other scavengers and to bring down large game, particularly deer, when there is a crust on deep snow that is strong enough to support a coyote but not a deer. We are good at adapting survival tactics. As parents, we work as a team to raise our offspring - usually six pups are born in April or May.

European settlers widely exterminated wolf populations in eastern North America and created an opportunity for us coyotes to extend our range. We began arriving in southern Ontario during the first quarter of the twentieth century. As it is everywhere else, we are also in perpetual conflict with farmers, even though they lose only a few of their livestock to coyotes. Early in our spread into new areas, we disregarded normality and bred together with remnants of wolf populations."

These unions have resulted in coyote races distinguished mostly by their larger size. Coyotes across Canada vary in size by as much as twelve kilograms. Hybrids, with their coyote-like adaptability, can survive, despite human persecution. They have evolved to become a true-breeding race.

"Pioneers, as well as many farmers today, saw and see me as a competitor and try to kill us off. City folk, who don't have the sense enough to keep their cats and little dogs in the house or on a restraint, want to put a bounty on my head. Well, go ahead if it makes you feel better. But, listen, it has been tried, and it doesn't work.

Yes, we are having a rough time of it now. Mother Nature knows that we are now too many, and with or without your involvement, our numbers' will soon be reducing to a sustainable population. If you feel you must take measures to rid yourself of coyotes, as a species we will prevail. Coyotes have evolved in a changing environment, which sometimes killed off many of us all at once. To help us recover, we are genetically programmed to have litters of up to sixteen pups; sexually mature at one year instead of two. And, coyote populations from outside your sphere of influence will move in to fill the void.

Some people say that we are too adaptable to human activity. Others see us as among the fortunate few that can live alongside humans. Give nature time to work its magic, and we will soon

MILE POST 104 AND BEYOND

again sleep beneath your backyard deck until all is quiet, before making a meal of that rabbit that has been eating your garden.

I am an expert at survival, and I remind you that the land is not yours alone. I received three howls from my country cousins. They ask me to thank the farmers for depositing dead livestock in the bush. Without their help, most of us would not have survived the winter. And yes, **please** keep that pest of a donkey in the barn."

Cheers,

Trickster Coyote

NATURAL RESOURCES - BEYOND BIOLOGICAL MANAGEMENT

The challenges facing us in the twenty- first century are here and now, and predicting the future can sometimes be a way of avoiding dealing with the problems of the present.

People who live in Canada's vast wilderness, the 'bush', are a colourful thread in the tapestry of Canadian history. What follow, are personal experiences, reminiscent of our life, far different from how most live today.

For many city dwellers, cut off from the reality of nature, the trapper is a person who kills animals – this is true. High fur prices in the 1930's and World War II years had trappers vigorously competing, without thought of conservation. Consequently, populations were reduced to such levels that survival of some species became threatened. This concern initiated the Registered Trapline Management System. All Crown Land Trappers were licensed to trap and to manage delineated areas, known as a Trapline, where they had exclusive trapping privileges. Conservation Officers conducted workshops, teaching fur-harvesters how to manage their Trapline for economic sustainability.

The Registered Trapline Management System worked. In the process, many non-native trappers came to understand that they too were part of that natural world and that over-trapping had consequences. The trapper, whatever opinion others have, is a person who has a place in the natural world. Aboriginal peoples have used and managed the natural environments in their territories long before the arrival of Europeans. They did so in their cultural belief, that, unlike other animals that we share our planet with, humans have the concept of time. We are not the boss, but the custodians. We are to use our intelligence, not to destroy that which supports us. Scientists have been warning mankind that survival, as we know it, is not possible if we do not bring to an end the damage we are doing to our environment.

As a trapper, hunter, fisher, and Conservation Officer, and with close association to traditional native culture (Teachings), I believe that traditional values are mankind's way to a sustainable future. The Registered Trapline Management System and education brought back sustainable wildlife populations and economy to a segment of our society, who, for the most part, were not academically educated; however they understood the fundamentals of survival. The trapper is but one example of how we can learn to live within the limitations of nature.

How well people manage life in the bush depends on how they see themselves in relation to the natural environment. If they view nature through a windowpane, their lives will be a never-ending struggle.

The challenge – Federal, Provincial and First Nations' management strategies for the years to come, I see going well beyond biological management. In a book called Future Hype: The Tyranny of Prophecy, Toronto sociologist, Max Dublin, warns that preoccupation with the future may make us neglectful of the lessons of the past. No matter how we want to control the future by our foresight, the unfolding of events is not inevitable. We can expect that much will remain unpredictable.

We should use common sense in developing a strategic plan, which will anticipate and plan for what is still over the horizon. Common sense is deeper, richer, and more powerful for thinking about the future, because it takes into account both experience and context. The world is changing, and leadership is being directly challenged by the changing values of individuals and communities. We don't have to be prophets to know that we must change to meet a new reality.

The twentieth century was a time of transition. The generation, whose values formed during the Great Depression and the Second World War, have changed. Taking its place was a generation whose evolving values were shaped in the counter-culture of the 1960s. They value individualism and do not follow leaders as uncritically as people in the past. There is an awakening of awareness to the environment and our natural resources. Many people are no longer willing to sit idly by and watch environmental abuse. Their expectations for quality of life have changed. Society is beginning to understand that our material comfort must not be at the expense of our environment – or of our children or our grandchildren.

In Canada, we are now a society made up of many diverse elements of race, language, age, income, and occupation, including minority groups, which are visible and invisible. Each of these groups has its needs and expectations in life.

As a person who considers wise natural resource management critical to all life, I see an urgent challenge to put natural resource management science into a context that can be appreciated by all people alike.

Can we not come together to talk and choose new a path? All of us have reached the point where we are questioning the way we are treating our one and only home – the planet Earth. People the world over are questioning the action and inaction of world leaders. First Nation communities are working towards a renewal – asking questions of their peers and elders, searching past knowledge abandoned along the pathways of years ago.

Here is a piece of 1984 Elder's advice regarding Natives' relationship with the natural world: "Treat the Earth and all of her aspects as your mother. Show deep respect for the Mineral World, the Plant World and the Animal World. Do nothing to pollute the air or soil. If others would destroy our mother; rise-up with wisdom to defend her."

RUSSIA - 1993

Inge and I decided to celebrate early retirement by visiting friends in Kazan, Russia. We met Professor Igor Paramonov when he was a visiting scholar at the University of Western Ontario, London, Ontario and his wife Mila on her visit to Canada. Igor had successfully competed with thousands of scholars from across the Soviet Union for one of the thirteen Exit Permits to study in Canada.

We had taken every opportunity to show Igor Canadian and American life including helping him to get a U.S. visa so he could travel with us to Atlanta, Georgia. Observing Igor's reaction to our extravagances made it obvious that life in Russia was different. Now, Igor and his family would show us their world.

With our passports stamped, official invitation by the Russian Embassy, we boarded an Aeroflot airline bound for a collapsing Soviet Union. We were off to visit the Paramonov family and see Russia.

A Siberian friend's parting words prepared us well. "If you don't need to take a shower or wash your hair every day, and if you make the effort to know the people, you will have a wonderful time. Like a set of Matrioshka dolls, Russia has many faces, so be careful, not to judge from your first impressions. Russia has endured a history of oppression so look for the beauty in the eyes of the people because they are the window to her soul". He was

MILE POST 104 AND BEYOND

right! He also helped us to secure our luggage with wire and ducttape to prevent airport pilferage.

Upon arrival at Moscow airport, we knew that we were in a different place. North American airport efficiency was absent. Instead, we saw systemic inefficiencies and corruption. We were now in a place where everyday life was a constant struggle. People earned extra money and favour from the customs agent extorting bribes to enter the country, train crews hand delivering mail and almost every vehicle on the street providing taxi service. Above it all, there was an unmistakable beauty – the people!

When I asked why adolescent boys would run up and touch me, I was told that it was because you are free, and they too want to be. This innocent gesture was the concept that freedom was in some way a quantifiable commodity worth the risk.

I saw two little girls, proudly and efficiently, selling lemonade. It appeared that people were buying lemonade from the little girls, not because they were thirsty, but because they could do so. I sensed great excitement and apprehensive anticipation due to the changes occurring. I am confident that the Russian people, given time, will change their history of oppression and make their dream of freedom a reality. It will not happen overnight or without struggle. But these enduring people will create a future much different from their centuries of oppression.

The Russian economy was in a shambles. The U.S. dollar/Russian ruble exchange rate was one to one thousand. The Paramonov family paid the equivalent of thirty-five U.S. cents a month rent for their small apartment while a can of Coca-Cola cost one U.S. dollar. A ride on the streetcar cost five kopecks, and there are one hundred kopecks in one Russian ruble. A bottle of vodka, without a replaceable top, cost eighty cents, while one with a replaceable top cost one dollar. I told Igor if the Soviets had exported their vodka bottle top technology instead of building rockets they just might have won the Cold War.

People everywhere greeted us with a smile, and they went to great effort to make us welcome. Without expectation, they offered their hospitality, and we accepted. We visited the city of Perm, which is located in the Ural Mountains 1,400 kilometers west of Moscow. In Soviet times, Perm was a major center of the Soviet Defence Industry and was off-limits to Westerners. Everywhere we traveled we were accompanied by two escort details. One group dressed as 1930's Al Capone mobsters while the other dressed as plain clothed police. We were free to go wherever we wished. We travelled in a caravan of brand-new imported cars. After Mila had advised me not to, I offered one of the drivers a $5.00 tip. He refused by showing me a one-inch wad of American one hundred dollar bills. Traveler lesson 101 – heed your host's advice when travelling in foreign lands.

Our Perm hosts took us to their dacha (country cottage) where we ate great food, took a Russian steam bath, and drank vodka. Although I escaped the steam bath heat with a plunge in the Babushka (Grandmother) River, prior Smirnoff training allowed me to stay the vodka course. An evening to remember!

As Inge picked strawberries, a lady from a neighboring cottage asked, in a U.S. mid-west accent, if she would like some fresh cream to go with her berries. When asked where she had learned to speak English so well, she said, "We had very good language schools in Perm". We had a similar experience walking down a street in the city of Gorky (renamed Nizhniy-Novgorod). A lady asked, in an American accent, if we would mail a letter to her friend in England when we got back to America. Taking her letter, I asked, in what country did you learn to speak English so well? She said, "I was language teacher in Siberia and have never been to any English speaking country; but, I hope to do so someday."

MILE POST 104 AND BEYOND

Our holiday drew to a close with a trip from Kazan to Moscow via a 1,000 kilometers Volga River boat cruise. Though the people were welcoming and wonderful, the sites along the way showed that the Soviet experiment had gone terribly wrong. We saw beautiful churches of an earlier time and an occasional pretty house, but it was evident that socialist communism ignored structural attractiveness. Depressing looking twenty story prefabricated concrete (Plattenbav) apartment blocks gave little incentive for urban tidiness. Leninism may have kindled a social awareness intending to end past wrongs. What happened here was unquestionably not in the best interest of their people.

People everywhere worked at restoring beautiful churches which in Soviet times they were used as warehouses. When we arrived at the Paramonov home people were celebrating neighbours having a telephone installed. The time from making the application to getting a telephone installed was several years. In Kazan, we saw a large statue of Lenin at one end of a street and at the other end there was a communal water pipe where people living on the street got their water.

July of 1993 was an interesting time to visit Russia. We witnessed the final Military Honour Guard ceremony at Lenin's tomb in Moscow's Red Square. Next doors, two newly rich Russians were buying a gold inlaid toilet at a recently opened store that would only accept payment in U.S. dollars or German marks. As we continued our tour of Moscow, we came upon brides placing their wedding bouquets on the Tomb of the Unknown Soldier. A beautiful Russian custom!

The most misleading Cold War misinformation was about 'big, ugly, Russian babushka wearing women pulling ploughs'. Quite to the contrary, as a seasoned admirer of pretty ladies, I can say there is only one way to describe Russian women – drop-dead-beautiful.

We came to know some very nice people and are forever grateful to the Paramonov family and their friends for hosting us. Thank you.

The Paramonovs - 2015 Epilogue:

In 1996 on a Moscow approved U.S. Fulbright Faculty Scholarship, Igor attended the University of Montana School of Business Administration. This time Igor was accompanied by his wife Mila, daughters Helen aged thirteen, and Jenny, aged eight. Extending their time one year, Igor taught International Business at the University. Mila, a Russian educated professional engineer, worked at lesser jobs while obtaining her U.S./Canadian Professional Certification and later was employed as an engineer. Helen and Jenny quickly mastered the English language and excelled at school.

In late 1997, the Paramonov family, granted Canadian Permanent Residency, moved to Calgary, Alberta. Igor is a Lecturer at the Southern Alberta Institute of Technology Business School. Mila is a leading Calgary Structural Engineer. Helen, Mrs. Del Bucchia, obtained her University of Calgary degree in Economics, and now owns a successful Interior Design Business in Calgary. Jenny completed her Harvard undergraduate degree, declined acceptance to Harvard Law in favour of furthering her education in Europe and Canada. She graduated the University of British Columbia in 2015 and will begin her law career in Toronto.

This high achievement family keeps in touch with relatives and friends in Russia. At the time of the Olympic games, these proud Canadians cheered their Russian roots and celebrated Canadian successes...

MILE POST 104 AND BEYOND

Grandfather Igor and Granddaughter Sophie
The first (Paramonov) to be born in Canada

MY GREATEST TEACHERS

Over the years, I have been privileged to have outstanding teachers, beginning with my parents and some excellent teachers during my formal education. More knowledge has also come to me from family, friends, and career. Being stuffed full of facts and skills is crucial to survival, but it is the ideas that set in place the framework of life. It is our human ability to perceive life that defines humanity – setting us apart from all other living creatures. Albert Einstein, the quintessential eccentric said: "Education is not the learning of facts, but the training of the mind to think."

Moochum Joe

My first great teacher was Moochum Joe. Most of my kind (white) thought him to be an illiterate, good-for-nothing, lazy, old "Indian". To me, Moochum Joe was a great loving friend, my most memorable of teachers. From his hours of monotone ramblings about great ancestral hunters and the forest spirits, I began to understand that we humans were neither more nor less than a part of nature; often confusing my limited understanding of my Christian upbringing, and putting me in trouble with my mother. Another lesson early learned; your strength will come from listening and thinking, rather than being so ready to tell people what you are thinking, or that, they might be wrong.

The pioneer belief held by most people in my youth was that the Canadian wilderness was a challenge to triumph over.

Pushing aside First Peoples, clearing away the trees, road building, and digging up the earth were seen as imperialistic and divine conquests with little or no consideration for our home – Planet Earth.

It was Moochum who taught me to see the wilderness as a complex community of life. Most often expressed as animals, fish, vegetation, and rocks – each one having its own unique but interdependent spirit and place of importance in nature. Like humans, all things in nature were put here by a greater power for one and each other's respectful use. That failure, to exercise proper respect, had consequences. Expressed as angering the Windigo Devil Spirit – not good, for bad things may come upon you. Windigo or not, just consider the mess we make of our environment.

Moochum would tell me, "People have the intelligence to change things; except for beavers, no other animals set about to change the territory. When you go in the bush, Bobby, you now know the way. If things go bad, you will only become scared when you don't think. You have everything you need to live – don't grow up like those white men who damage Mother Earth. Nabis (boy), there is another way – always remember people are not the boss". That other way, I came to realize, is that man's role is that of a custodian of the natural world and not Master.

Moochum thought enough of a little white boy to pass along the wisdom of his culture – a gift.

Dr. John Dale and Jean Owen

It was they, who gave me one of the greatest gifts I've ever received. They taught me to be grateful for what I had. They showed me there are great hidden blessings in our lives, if only we open our minds and our hearts to the world around us.

John (Jack) Owen was his own man. He did his own thing, oblivious to the conventions or practicalities of the day. His passionate curiosity set his course for diverse and colossal collections and knowledge. Aside from his successful medical practice, he collected three steamer trunks of uncirculated U.S. postage stamps and eighteen thousand phonograph records. With gardener, Charley Zehner's help, planted ten thousand tulip bulbs on their estate home property, and annually, grew thousands of flowers from seed, in his friend's greenhouse. His eccentric ways had our driveway full of cars, as he would not be bothered to trade in his old cars when acquiring a new vehicle. After his retirement, he went on to collect Navajo art and pottery – then rocks. Jack Owen's rocks became his most colossal of collections. His passionate ways set him on the thankfully failed course to collect every semi-precious stone and rock on the planet.

Dr. Owen's obstetric medical practice was renowned; he pioneered the relationships between diet, pregnancy, and childbirth. Dr. John Dale Owen died in 1980.

The totality of Dr. Owen's teaching was best summarized in a commencement speech given by an unknown professor: "When life gives you 100 reasons to cry, show life that you have 1,000 reasons to smile. Face the past without regret. Handle your present with confidence. Prepare for the future without fear. It is your personal adventure – live it full-tilt. There are a lot of things that are worse than failure."

Phillip Sawdo

Phillip Sawdo was my third greatest teacher. It was from Phillip's example (Phillip Sawdo Cries) that I learned we had the capacity and strength to put aside 'the bad and the ugly,' to move forward, and to live a better day. And!

My Little Dog, Bernie

Bernie gave me her unconditional love. She was very intelligent in ways much different than humans. I never spoke harsh or spoke loud to her, as she was not deaf, and it would confuse her sensitivities. Her aim was always to please, and that she did. When hunting, she was always at my side. My slow two-finger hand gesture would make her still, no matter how excited she was and wanting to give an instinctive chase. If I were to be away for more than two days, Bernie would take food from my mother only, but no one else.

In summary

My greatest teachers neither deliver their lessons from behind a podium nor were they always crafted in well-defined words. They were the gifts of ideas – examples of life to be mulled over in the mind. There may have been other 'great teachers' whose ideas I missed, as they did not fit my personality or my comprehension. One will never know!

Acts of kindness can change a life.

THE LAST PERIOD . . .

I began this project by saying that I was doing so without an outline. I also told about an artist friend staring at a blank wall and a clean canvas on her easel and my asking, "What are you about to paint?" She replied, "I don't know – we will have to wait and see what develops". This same friend also said that the most difficult thing for an artist is to know when to put the brush down and sign their name to the creation. I believe the same to be true for a novice author like myself. Where do you place that last 'period'?

It was my intention to not write an autobiography. It appears, however, in large part, that I have, and why not close some family circles?

My brother Jim lived with the Owens in Milwaukee for ten years. Upon graduating from the University of Wisconsin he joined the U.S. Army and retired twenty-five years later as a full colonel. During his military career, he served in Germany and Vietnam. Jim died in 2002 from ALS. We suspect his early demise may have been brought on as the result of being exposed to "unknowns" during his role as, as he would say, "Military advisor in Vietnam".

Remember The Day Jacky Got Born? John is what I like to refer to as an "imaginative thinker". Having no practical idea as to how mechanical things work, John has gone on to invent and manufacture new and revolutionary equipment for the medical field. His imagination and passion for art have led him to establish a one-of-a-kind art gallery in Tucson, Arizona. Fifty-seventy thousand square feet of gallery space dedicated not to the end product but the creation of art and the impassioned struggle of the artist. John — you make a difference.

The youngest brother George also lives in Tucson, Arizona. Unlike John, George has to know how everything mechanical works. George's life has been automobiles, his wife Karen, and their six girls. Not in that order, of course.

In the mid-1950s, Mother and Dad moved to Arizona with John and George to manage the Owens' Sierra Vista Guest Ranch. Dad later returned to the lakes and trees in North-western Ontario. Our parents died in the 1980's.

The Owens also died in the l980's, having spent their many retirement years at their Sierra Vista ranch. Doctor Jack had many interests during his retirement—avid gardener, archaeologist, rock hound, as well as helping to establish the Emergency Medical Technician program in Arizona. His wife, Jean, did much of Jack's legwork and was an accomplished watercolour artist.

To the many wonderful people whose lives touched mine and whom I have written about, and, to the many others, whose tales need telling at another time. I say, "**thank you**".

ACKNOWLEDGEMENTS

It is customary to state that the author could not have done so without the usual list of past and present contributors... Not as obvious are the many friends and acquaintances that endured my storytelling... 'You should write a Book'... (they'd say)

I would not have undertaken this project if it were not for the encouragement of family and friends:

- In particular Gerard (Jerry) Wyatt, Professor Emeritus (Yale and Queen's University)
- Al Morid and Rachel Doucet-Wells for the sketches.
- Philippe Baud for photographic expertise.
- Albert DeLaat for his computer skills.
- Perry Wells, Jon Wintrop, Don and Helen McQuat for editing my scribbles into conventional readable English.
- My brother John for story recollections.
- Kenn M. Feigelman, Director of Operations Deep/Quest 2 Explorations for the hours he spent editing and proofreading my revised transcript.
- Especially Brian Cameron for his patience to review writing written rotten.

I thank my wife, Inge, for her encouragement and **help** during this project. Much love!

Thank you.

Bobby Wells – From Mile Post 104

Edwards Brothers Malloy
Oxnard, CA USA
July 7, 2015